AF575287

Stephen Bush

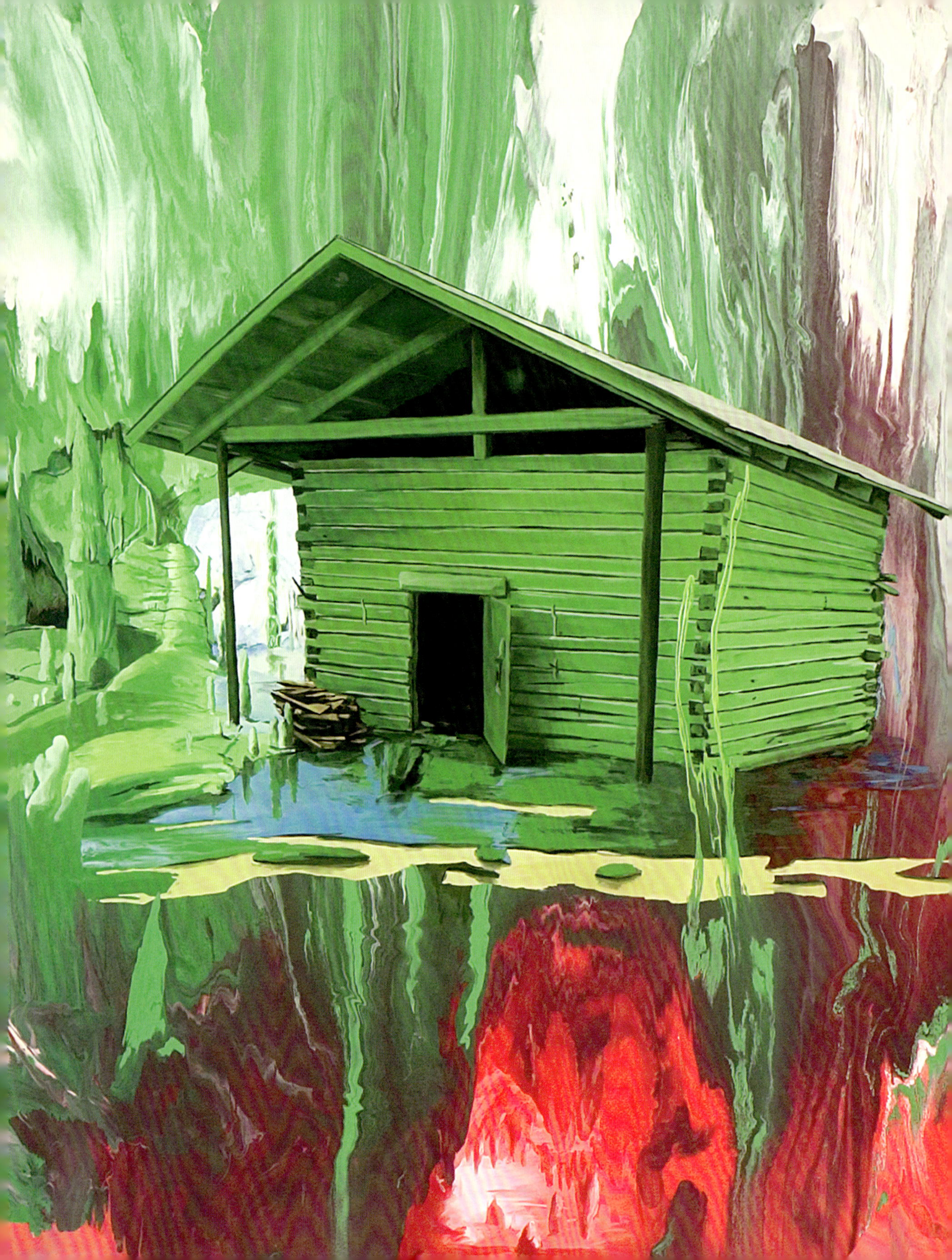

Stephen Bush

GELDERLAND

SITE SANTA FE

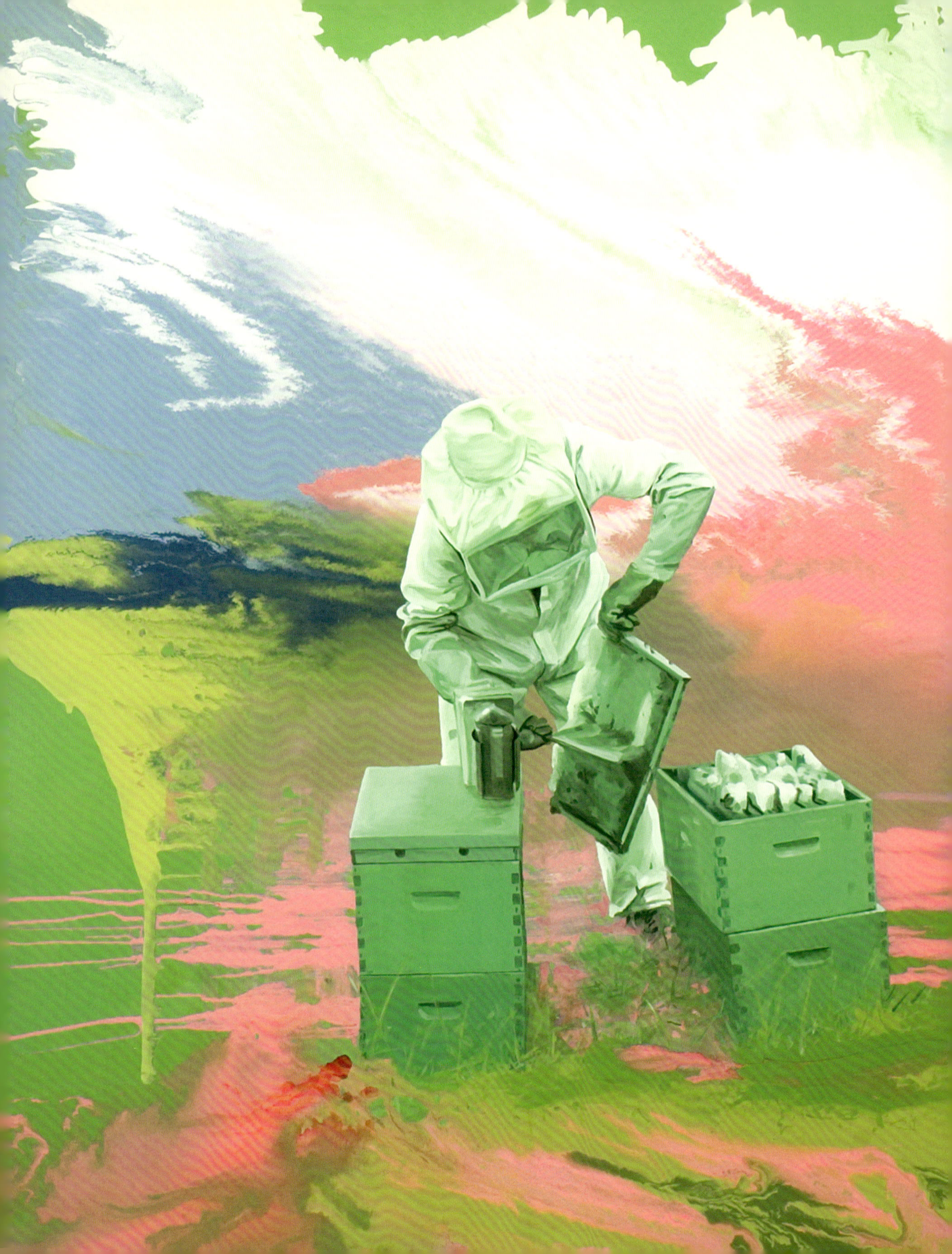

contents

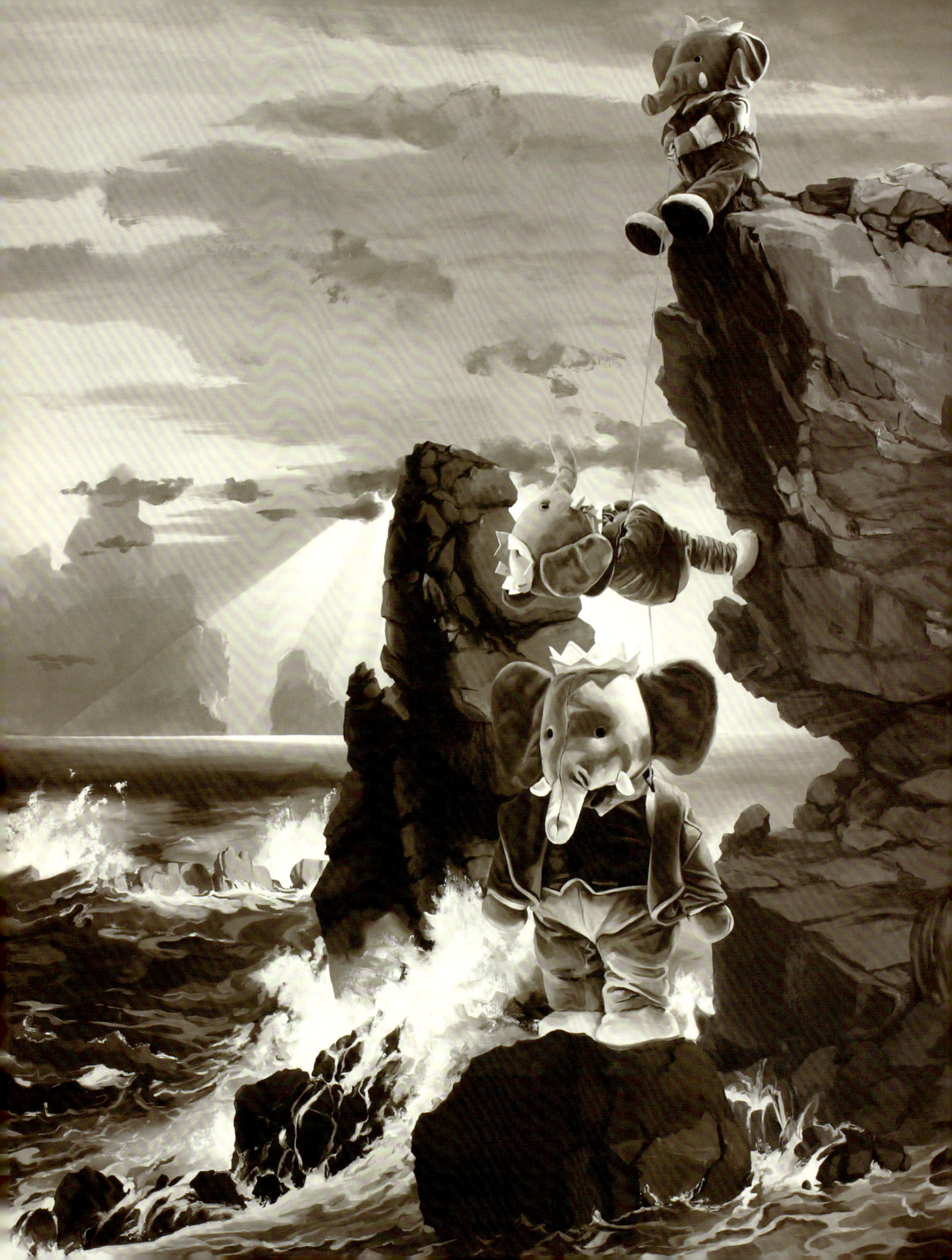

foreword

Laura Steward Heon
Director/Curator

STEPHEN BUSH'S PAINTINGS STAYED IN MY HEAD like an unshakable tune from the first moment I saw them in a collector's house in 2002. I had gone to see the work of a different artist, but Bush's paintings kept pulling my gaze away from the ones I was supposed to be looking at. Embarrassingly, I promptly forgot Bush's name, which forced me to spend the next several years searching high and low, asking anyone I could if they knew of a painter whose works fit the description of the ones that had captivated me. When they finally popped up again, at Goff + Rosenthal Gallery in New York, I did not hesitate to offer Bush a show here at SITE Santa Fe.

Bush has a complicated and large oeuvre. He follows his varied enthusiasms — for the children's book character Babar, French academic painting, American regionalist painting, extreme techniques, beekeepers — with intoxicating relentlessness, probing every painterly possibility they offer to the utmost before moving on to the next. Liza Statton, Thaw Curatorial Fellow, bravely gives chase in her illuminating essay in this catalogue, and Ashley Crawford, an Australian like Bush, provides insight into a constant underlying concern that is not so apparent to a U.S. audience — namely Bush's dedication to examining the post-colonial condition in their country.

I am indebted to Liza Statton and Joanne Lefrak, SITE Santa Fe's Curatorial Coordinator, for their tenacity, intelligence, and good humor in tracking down paintings and bringing this catalogue, the first on Bush's work in the U.S., into being. Goff + Rosenthal Gallery, representing Bush in the U.S., and Bush's longtime Australian representative, Sutton Gallery, have been very supportive of the exhibition. Particular thanks must go to Phoebe Dougall, the director of the Sutton Gallery, who has done yeoman's duty. She has been in nearly daily contact with SITE for several months from the other side of the world. SITE is also grateful to Arts Victoria for generously underwriting the shipping costs of works coming from Australia.

Finally, the staff and Board of SITE Santa Fe must thank Stephen Bush himself for agreeing to this exhibition. He has been a thoughtful and responsive collaborator, and we are very proud to be the first to present his extraordinary work in depth to a U.S. audience.

Metaphor, Melancholia and Mayhem

by Ashley Crawford

AUSTRALIA, LIKE THE USA, IS A POST-COLONIAL SOCIETY. Like America it is a land of dramatically differing topography, ranging from lush forests to harsh deserts. Like America it is a country where the indigenous people have largely been thrown off their land, the early British settlers destroying ancient cultures with nary a shrug. Where the two countries differ dramatically, apart from odd marsupials and weird accents, is the fact that Australia began its 'Western' life as a penal colony.

Australia was 'discovered' by Captain James Cook on February 26, 1770. Dubbed *Terra Australis* it was claimed for the Crown of England. The presence of native people was dismissed as an inconvenience and the likelihood of Spanish and Chinese explorers beating Cook to finding the continent has long been an issue of academic dispute. The upshot is that the English decided to use this far-away land as a penal colony — a remote prison where the rabble could be sent to serve out the terms of their natural lives. Thus the early Australian settlers were murderers and thieves and pickpockets along with eccentrics and explorers. Many of them were Irish, which is in essence, Stephen Bush's ancestry. Such a bloodline makes sense when one considers the Irish love of a good story, and with the narratives implicit in Bush's paintings it is clear that he is a natural born storyteller.

Bush has become well known in his home country for his heroic portrayal of Babar the Elephant in *The Lure of Paris* [**PLATE 22**] series. These paintings are the result of the happy accident of Bush finding a stuffed toy Babar on the street. Babar's existence began in 1931 as a popular children's story in *L'Histoire de Babar* by Jean de Brunhoff. English language versions appeared in 1933 in Britain and the United States. In the story, after Babar's mother was killed by a hunter in Africa he finds his way to Paris. Babar eventually returns to the jungle to 'civilize' his fellow elephants. It is a post-colonial story *par excellence*. Babar dresses his fellow elephants in suits in much the same way that British colonials dressed the American Indian and Australian Aboriginal in order to 'civilize' them. Bush takes this a step further in his paintings by depicting Babar venturing along rugged coastlines, discovering new lands and 'civilizing' them. As Jonathan Goodman, writing in *Art in America* in 1997, so aptly put it: "Bush's archly postmodern send-ups of epic historical paintings are so tongue-in-cheek one nearly forgets how well painted they are." [1]

Even a beekeeper becomes a post-colonial despot in Bush's world, reigning-in that most civilized of insects, the bee. The images in the *Caretaker* series vary dramatically but they share a strangely other-worldly air; the hooded figure thoroughly incongruous in the landscape which itself refers to 17th Century Dutch *landschap* painting and its imposition on the Australian bush that was so much a part of the colonial experience.

Indeed, much colonial-era landscape painting in Australia was used to entice British settlers to inhabit this newfound 'Eden.' The harshness of the real bushland was softened in color and tone. In effect, when sent back to England, these paintings acted as real-estate advertising; the cash-strapped British government had realized that rather than treat Australia as a gigantic prison, they could make a great deal of money by selling large swathes of would-be farmland. The realities of the difficulty of cultivating this rough continent were obliterated under the painters' bristles.

Things get even weirder when Bush turns up the volume on his palette, seen in such violently shuddering works as *Jaune de Nickel* (2003) [PLATE 19], where the caretaker seems to struggle in an irradiated landscape. This is post-apocalyptic — it makes no sense as a rational picture — but again Bush paints it with such technical flair and gleeful exuberance that somehow it works.

In true post-colonial style, Bush is a specialist in making the mundane miraculous by juxtaposing the surreal with the real, creating a palimpsest between abstraction and the representational. He has rendered humble farm tractors as heroic machines and painted majestically gigantic potatoes. There has always been something of the surreal mixed with the regal in his early work, largely rendered in an old-world sepia palette, seen in *The Lure of Paris* paintings.

Bush creates an entirely new world in recent works such as *Ericifolia* (2005) [**PLATE 5**]. This new world is one of rustic retreats set amidst swirling, abstracted Alpine mountain-scapes and mind-shattering skies. His clapboard cabins, clearly built with the rugged do-it-yourself approach of Grizzly Adams, are painted in an almost realistic style, but the skies above are purely crazed abstractions — a hallucinogenic tsunami of broiling color.

There can be little doubt that Bush is playing with the viewer when he titles his works with such wonderfully mundane, greeting-card-style names as *Southeast in the Summer* (2006), *Brighten My Northern Sky* (2004), or *Gripped Me Goldly* (2004). These deliberately evoke a Mills and Boone-style romanticism, but are in fact taken from the more *outré* songs of such contemporary musicians as Will Oldham and Nick Drake. The titles may suggest sentimentalism, but both the music and the paintings they have inspired, suggest anything but. The paintings brood with portent, suggestive of the fact that no matter how we cling to the land — in a colonialist sense or any other way — nature will have her way.

Writing in *Artforum* magazine Nell McClister noted that "what was quiet and meditative becomes shrieking and ominous, the sublime depiction of majestic topography twisted into garish chemical goo . . . . Bush turns some of the landscape genre's central terms inside out. Rather than a mind calmed by the natural environment, these paintings record the external manifestation of psychological trauma."[2] In some of Bush's paintings one is reminded of mystical Eastern retreats, in others of a faraway existence surrounded by Alpine majesty. Placing his structures in a malformed unnatural maelstrom, Bush manages to portray a sense of humanity and survival, spirituality and awe in the face of an overwhelming and alien nature.

The contrasts in style in any one canvas are what make these paintings so jarring. The coloration is achieved by the unusual mix of oil paint and enamel to create an almost transcendental gloss — a sky can be a garish marbled pink juxtaposed against the greens of his figurative landscapes. When he wanders into the Alpine mountains and the swamplands these contrasts become explicit; the real and the unreal sit in uneasy alliance. Many later works are named after a species of plant, grounding the more hallucinogenic elements of the paintings in terra firma. But it is the contrast of approaches that gives pause; the restful and solitary environs seem to be psychological barriers against a tumultuous world that shimmers and shifts above.

One work that isn't named after a species of flora is *Sure Nuff Yes I Do* (2004) [**PLATE 8**], the title lifted from a classic Captain Beefheart song from the 1970 album *Safe as Milk*. Looking at this work it's safe to assume that Bush is a Beefheart fan; both the artist and the band share a fondness for the surreal and for the juxtaposition of the guttural and the poetic, the visceral and the sublime. In this regard Bush is also a 'pop' artist. His works, especially in their pigmentation, reflect the times in which he has lived. His shift from the muted palette of *The Lure of Paris* series to the glaring, almost neon hues of *Citriodora* (2005) [**PLATE 4**] or *Vert Or* (2004) [**PLATE 16**] recall the scintillating shift for his generation from black and white television to color. In his youth, growing up on a farm, he would have glimpsed the black and white album covers of his parents' Glenn Miller albums. At art school he would have witnessed the larger-than-life performances of Nick Cave, who also attended a Melbourne art school.

Similarly, like most of his generation, learning about visual art was via the rather stagnant Gombrich's *The Story of Art* with its dubious black and white reproductions. However, in Bush's formative years Robert Hughes burst out of the box with the colorful television program *The Shock of the New*, a show that Bush says made "connections between art and society and revealed a relationship to what is happening around us."[3] These broader cultural shifts — from muted grays and blacks and whites of the media of his youth, to the florid, neon, color-saturated world of today are reflected in his entire oeuvre. Bush has moved on from his somewhat cynical, albeit beautifully executed, fascination for the 'heroic' in art, expanding his language to create strange, almost surrealist paintings of man-made structures in lurid chroma. They are somewhat *Hansel and Gretel* — well after the witch has had her day.

Much of this shift has to do with materiality. In 2003, after a major survey exhibition, Bush felt that his concentration on form may have been becoming moribund and decided to treat paint "as liquid" — thus leaving room for accident. This approach, with his more formalized skill as a figurative painter, has created a unique, bizarre, almost schizophrenic combination of technique.

Bush has captured the spirit of the times in an eccentric but powerful way. His use of color is garish, his subjects at times almost medieval. But somehow these works dig beneath the surface of the psyche. Whereas beforehand his palette was muted, in more recent works it explodes. Despite the hallucinogenic mayhem, elements of nostalgia and melancholia pervade these works. His Babar is an explorer of old new-world adventurism; his log cabins are those of rugged mountain settlers, yet the results feel demandingly, indeed urgently, contemporary.

[1] Jonathan Goodman, "Stephen Bush at Fotouhi Cramer – New York," *Art in America*, January, 1997, p.128.
[2] Nell McClister, "Stephen Bush," *Artforum*, January, 2006, pp. 223-24.
[3] Conversation with the author, November, 2006

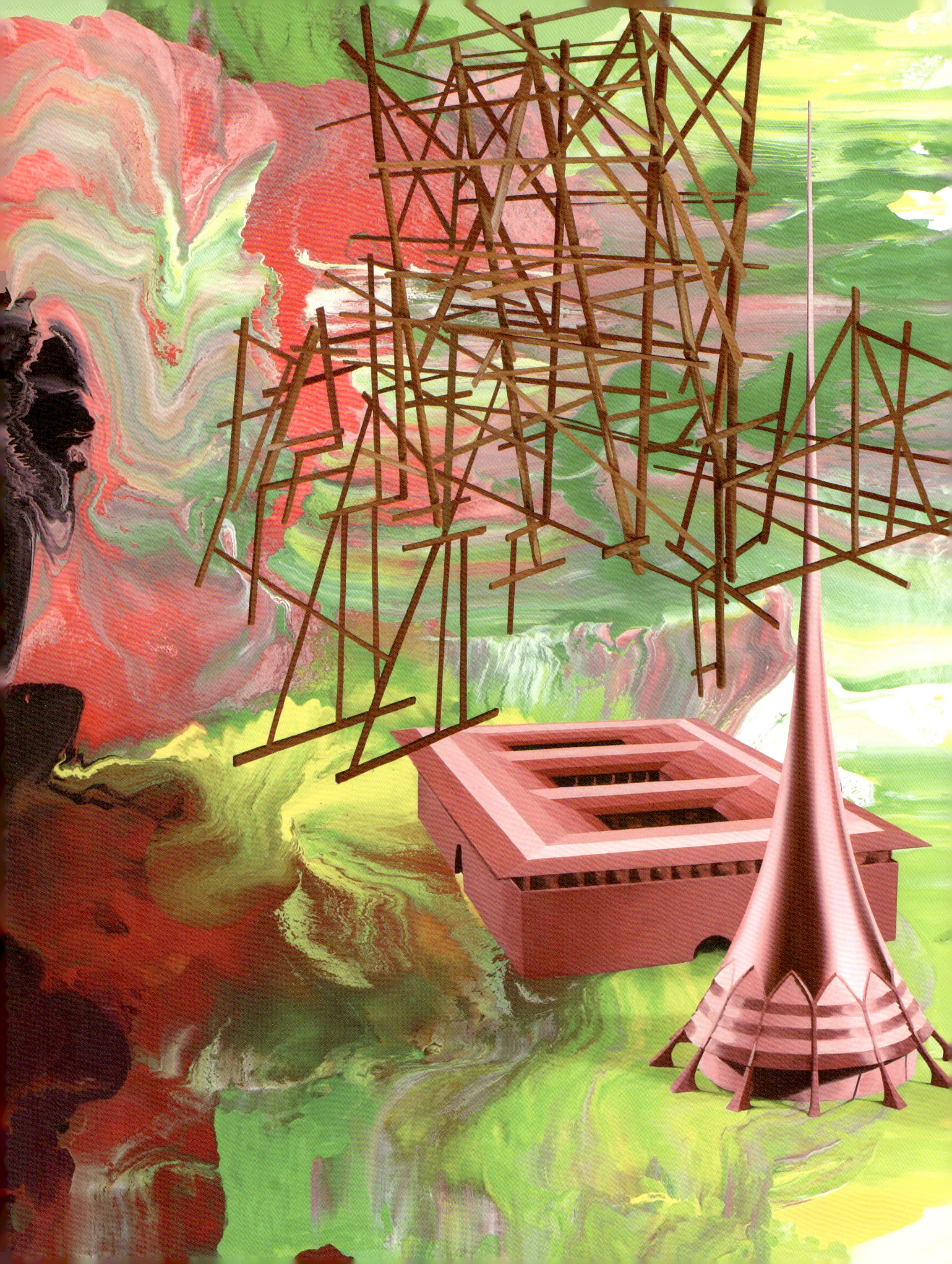

No Consolation Prizes

by Liza Statton

RARE IS THE ARTIST WHO CAN DEFTLY MELD SUBJECTS as disparate as Jean-Auguste-Dominique Ingres, nineteenth-century American painting, Andy Warhol, beekeepers, and Babar, to name but a few, into provocative, rather than kitsch-laden works of art. Yet, Australian painter Stephen Bush does so with wit and ease. What unites his seemingly discordant enthusiasms is a workman-like grappling with technique, and his devotion to process is at the core of his artistic project. Consider that Bush has painted *The Lure of Paris* [**PLATE 22**] twenty-seven times. Yes, that's correct, for more than a decade Bush has painted the exact same image of the children's storybook character Babar and his mountaineering mates rappelling down from the craggy cliffs above a threatening coastline. What's more, Bush paints each one of the *Lures* — only assigned numbers and dates distinguish the works from one another — from memory. Using only two tubes of paint, black and white, Bush paints the entire image as he remembers it at that particular moment. In effect, *The Lure of Paris* series becomes for Bush both a physical and conceptual game of hide-and-seek — albeit one with a custom-made set of rules — and a virtuosic display of his own technical proficiency.

The differences between individual paintings in the series are not obvious. Viewers must spend an immense amount of time looking at one work and then comparing it to another, and then again to another, and so on in order to detect *something* that differentiates the paintings. Bush's visual clues are remarkably subtle: for example, the uneven bands of clouds blanketing the overhead sky may have varying densities of gray, or the brilliant shaft of sunlight puncturing the background sky may not highlight the same expanse of water seen on the horizon, or the Babars, in their form-fitting velvet suits, sometimes appear to fluctuate in weight. In light of such details, the paintings gradually become entangled in an observational sport akin to *I-Spy* or *Where's Waldo?* Bush sets his viewers on a demanding, seemingly endless journey looking for clues, a crafty move that lures us into analyzing the formal qualities of the picture rather than contemplating the content of it.

Such a display of fancy footwork does not mean, however, that *The Lure of Paris* series is devoid of content, quite the contrary. Writing on the subject of post-colonial identity in *The Lure of Paris* and other works by Bush, contributing author Ashley Crawford addresses how Bush identifies with the figure of Babar as a Western cultural icon that embodies the dual roles of both the colonizer, France, and the subject of colonization, Africa. Moreover, the piece touches on Bush's wily juxtaposition of figural elements; Babar, originally the product of sharp lines and bold, flat patches of color constructed from the visual language of graphic illustration, is transposed into the muted *grisaille* evocative of Ingres, and set within a romantic landscape rendered in the guise of J.M.W. Turner. Indeed, the apparent incongruity between Babar and his surrounding environment points to the powerful absurdity of the entire scene, suggesting that Bush has a decidedly antagonistic rapport with any prescribed notions of "tradition."

Bush is perfectly content to leave viewers with any perceptual "meaning" of *The Lure of Paris* unresolved. It is unclear as to whether or not he's embracing the classical traditions of European academic painting or plainly thumbing his nose at them. Despite his ambivalence, questions persist: Why does Bush continue to paint the same picture over and over again? What does this repetition mean? And, where does this utter relentlessness and obsession with technique and process come from?

In addition to the subjects of post-colonial identity and tradition about which *The Lure of Paris* alludes, often with subtle wit and irony, the series also speaks to the physical and emotional rigors of the painting process. These paintings are, simply put, a reflection of

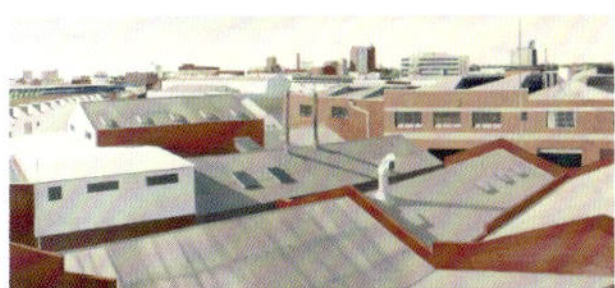

FIG. 1

Kings Way, 1982
Oil on canvas, 38 x 76 inches
City of Melbourne Art and Heritage Collection
Melbourne, Australia

Bush's pure, unadulterated manual labor, and this ethos of labor permeates his work in a powerful way. Unraveling the tangled mass of threads that form the basis of Bush's artistic process involves digging into the foundations of his rigid self-discipline, as well as examining the representational strategies of color, repetition, and juxtaposition that Bush employs in order to create thrilling, evocative paintings that strike a tenuous balance between subject matter and technique, tradition and innovation, and desire and ambition.

The origins of the controlled discipline that informs Bush's artistic process derives in part from growing up on his family's farm in Pennyroyal, near the rural town of Colac, Victoria. One of six children, Bush spent much of his youth and spare time working on the land. Tractor driving, sheep tending, and haymaking were just a few of his many labor-intensive activities. As he says, "Sounds a tad naf or romantic or both, but growing up on a farm was what you did, and when I grew up, everyone belonged to a large farming family.... This all sounds like a scene from the Walton's."[1] Farm work by its very nature involves direct contact with the land. It is often a solitary activity that is characterized by persistent redundancy — consider for a moment that farmers milk dairy cows every morning whether they want to or not.

The relentless repetition inherent in agricultural labor also describes the process of screen-printing — a medium that Bush came to know well as he taught courses on the subject while completing his post-graduate work at the Royal Melbourne Institute of Technology in 1979. Generally speaking, screen-printing is a complex process of layering and duplication. As it had for Andy Warhol, whose serialized use of Brillo boxes, Campbell Soup cans, and lurid depictions of Marilyn Monroe thoroughly emptied these cultural icons of their denotative meaning, the medium's versatility held great appeal for Bush. The process similarly allowed him to merge the formal and conceptual elements of painting and photography into imagery that spoke the visual language of popular culture.

Moreover, the screen-printing process accords the artist a certain distance between himself and the object being produced, and this sense of detachment is manifest in early works such as *Kings Way* (1982) **[FIG. 1]**, in which Bush renders Melbourne's urban topography through a series of rooftops. This stark, realistic scene is a study of light, color, and form. Sharp lines that define large, flat areas of muted color—essentially reduced to variegated tones of red, white, and blue—constitute the painting's figural elements. The unusual lighting heightens the lonely mood that permeates the picture, and the cropped, horizontal composition, drawn from the framing devices characteristic of photography and film, adds to this effect of detachment.

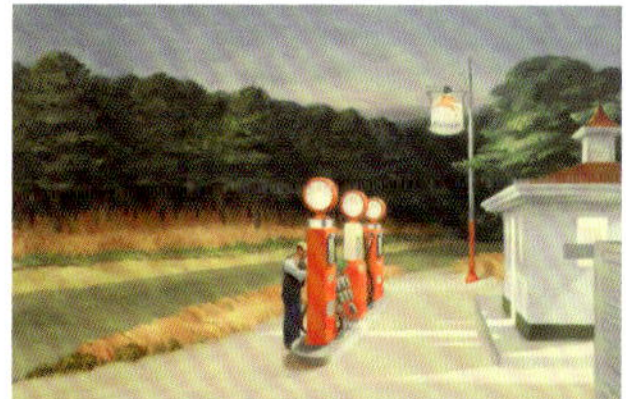

FIG. 2

Hopper, Edward (1882-1967)
Gas, 1940
Oil on canvas, 26 ¼ x 40 ¼ inches
Mrs. Simon Guggenheim Fund. (577.1943)
The Museum of Modern Art, New York, NY, U.S.A.
Digital Image © The Museum of Modern Art
Licensed by SCALA / Art Resource, NY

In *Yellow* (1984) **[PLATE 27]**, Bush depicts a similarly realistic scene of an empty construction site. Using bold patches of yellow, orange, green, and red, he transforms this industrial scene into an image worthy of deeper contemplation. Works such as *Yellow* and *Kings Way* with their deft coloration, formal clarity, detached mood, and cinematic feel speak to the influence of Edward Hopper. Paintings such as *Gas* (1940) **[FIG. 2]**, are emblematic of Hopper's formalist investigations and his realistic depictions of urban and rural life in America during the 1940s that captured the solitude of contemporary existence.

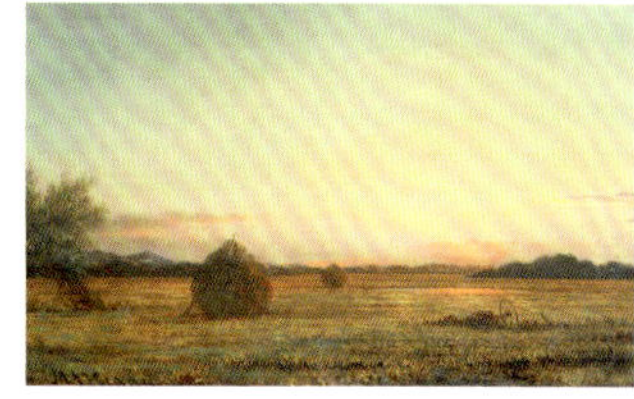

FIG. 3

Jersey Meadows (oil on canvas)
by Heade, Martin Johnson (1819-1904)
© Private Collection / © Christie's images
The Bridgeman Art Library

In the early 1980s, Bush was drawn to Hopper's Ashcan realism, use of color, and to the notion of the quotidian sublime—a theme Hopper deftly threaded throughout narrative works such as *House by the Railroad* (1926) and *Nighthawks* (1942). The idea that beauty can be found in the mundane was likewise integral to the art and philosophy of Andy Warhol, and it became central to the ethos of American pop art, which also spoke to Bush early in his career. However, after returning from an eight-month long, Kerouac-esque journey through the United States in 1984, Bush began to paint pictures that eschewed Hopper's cool realism and embraced the naturalism and theatricality found in nineteenth-century American photography and landscape painting.

In the luminous meadows of Martin Johnson Heade **[FIG. 3]**, the gritty voyageurs of George Caleb Bingham **[FIG. 4]**, and the prolific historic portraits of Charles Willson Peale, Bush located the origins of the quotidian sublime. The landscape and genre paintings by these unheralded American painters were not the stuff of "grand narrative" pictures rendered in the guise of the French academic heavyweights such as Poussin, Gericault, and

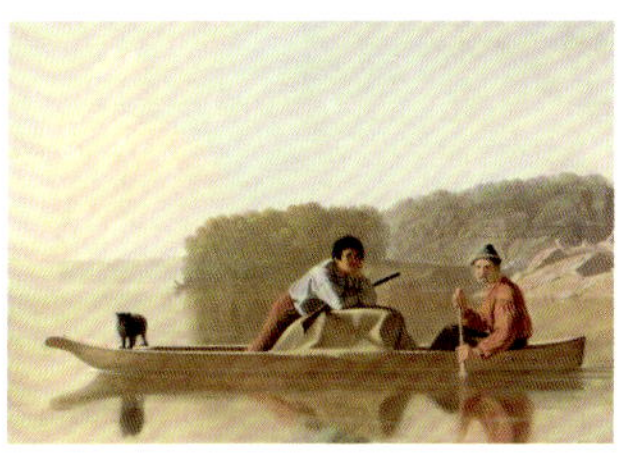

FIG. 4

The Trapper's Return, 1851 (oil on canvas)
by Bingham, George Caleb (1811-79)
© The Detroit Institute of Arts, USA
Gift of Dexter M. Ferry Jr. / The Bridgeman Art Library

Delacroix — the canonical figures they had come to know via Paris. Instead, these scrappy, peripatetic American artists created paintings that were filled with a profound sense of nationalistic pride and a determinist attitude that had sloughed off the burden of European "tradition." Their influence soon segued into Bush's work, blotting out his earlier enthusiasm for Hopper and Warhol.

Consider Bush's *Caretakers* paintings, from which his current series of *Beekeepers* derives. Each depicts the radiant, honey-colored figure of a beekeeper toiling away in an empty romantic landscape that Bush appropriated from George Caleb Bingham's genre pictures. A comparison between Bush's *A Caretaker #1* (1988) **[FIG. 5]** and Bingham's *The Trapper's Return* (1851) **[FIG. 4]** reveals the artist's appropriation of Bingham's Missouri River backdrop. At first glance at *A Caretaker #1*, it's easy to overlook the incongruity of the flamboyant beekeeper in relation to his surrounding environment — apparently the beekeeper's gold-colored suit was inspired by the one worn by Elvis Presley in his 1969 comeback tour. In *A Caretaker #2* (1988) **[PLATE 24]**, for example, we see the beekeeper tending his hive atop a mountain plateau, and *A Caretaker #3* (1988) **[PLATE 25]** depicts another caretaker laboring under the faint glow of a moonlit sky. The *Caretakers*, with their Elvis-inspired apiarist and nineteenth-century mid-Western settings, reflect an odd set of artistic choices — connecting the dots between the beekeeper, George Caleb Bingham, and Elvis Presley isn't easy. Yet, as with *The Lure of Paris*, Bush's technical proficiency reigns in the disparate subject matter, suggesting that there is something more to these works than mere rhapsodic musings on American art.

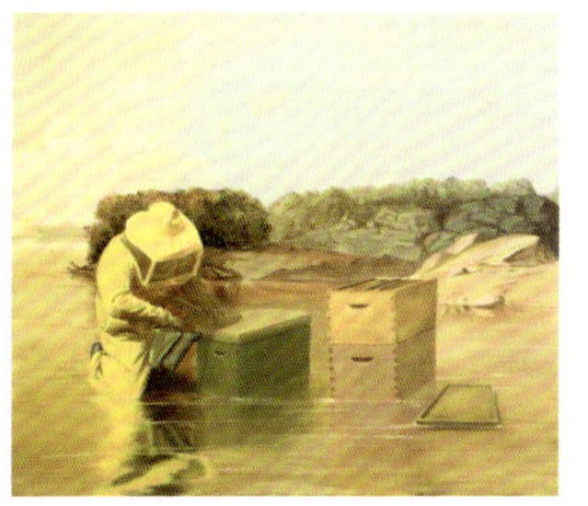

FIG. 5

Stephen Bush
A Caretaker #1, 1988
Oil on linen, 24 x 28 inches
Collection of John L. Stewart, New York, NY

Bush painted the *Caretakers* series during a period in the late 1980s when new media and appropriation art dominated much of the contemporary art scene. To be a figurative painter at the time was to be an outlier, and *Caretakers,* with its hermetic beekeeper, is perhaps both an apt metaphor for Bush's position at the time, as well as an ironic take on the conventions of appropriation art. Unlike many appropriation artists who employed media-based imagery to reveal the mechanics of social conditioning that television and advertising engendered, Bush ransacked the seemingly naive and peripheral art of such unlikely figures as George Caleb Bingham in order to paint pictures that challenged the historical legacy and relevance of the European academic tradition.

Despite their quiet quirkiness, *Caretakers* is a pivotal body of work that marks Bush's turn away from painting driven by subject matter toward a direct engagement with process. Technical elements such as paint facture, repetition, juxtaposition, and a reduction of color become the focus of Bush's attention throughout much of the 1990s, and his *Venetian Red* and *Pomme de Terre* series are emblematic of his shift in thought. In the *Venetian Red* [**FIG. 6**] series, for example, Bush reduced the mechanics of painting down to a simple tube of "Venetian Red" color that he used to paint recycled images of farm equipment, potatoes, insects, and beehives, among others. For this series, Bush concentrated on production, constraining himself to painting these random subjects in one day. *Pomme de Terre* [**FIG. 7**], a series based upon repeated images of Parisian rubbish bins, is similarly characterized by Bush's use of monochrome — in this case emerald green — that emphasizes the physical and conceptual process of painting.

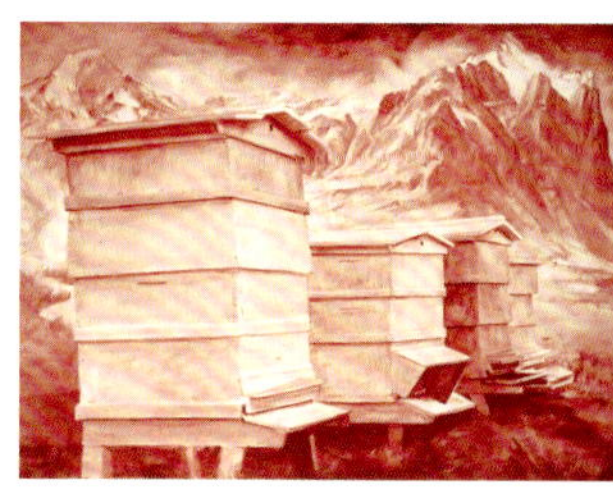

FIG. 6

Venetian Red #2, 1995
Oil on linen, 36 x 42 inches
Private collection, Melbourne, Australia

Toward the end of the 1990s, Bush begins to employ a more lurid, technicolor palette composed of electric pinks, purples, and magentas. His focus on process and materiality becomes even more apparent in his large-scale, roseate *I Have Come to the Creek* (2003) [**PLATE 18**]. Skeins of pink and magenta-colored paint slide behind the weird mass of tentacle-like forms that dominates the composition. Bush has said that the sculpted figure derives from reducing a group of clay models back down to the clay itself. Here the painting process, and the physicality of paint, take center stage. The impressions in the clay formed by his physical manipulation of the material echo the tactility and viscosity of the poured paint. Works like *I Have Come to the Creek* speak to Bush's shift in color and emerging interest in the juxtaposition between abstract and figural elements.

Since 2003, Bush has developed a penchant for creating apocalyptically-colored, volatile landscapes such as *Lauterbrunnental* (2004) [**PLATE 13**] and *Brighten My Northern Sky* (2004) [**PLATE 9**]. Emblematic of his desire to relinquish dictatorial control imposed by the

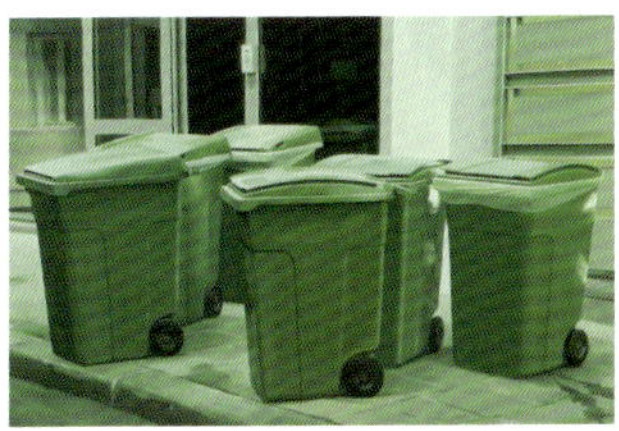

FIG. 7

Pomme de Terre #8, 2001
Oil on linen, 31 x 47 inches
Sutton Gallery, Melbourne, Australia

paintbrush, these works are executed through a process of pouring and spilling a mixture of enamel and oil paint directly onto the canvas. In contrast to Bush's obsession with displaying his satiric mastery, or "mimicry," of traditional European academic techniques, as in *The Lure of Paris*, chance and spontaneity ultimately determine the pictorial forms that emerge in paintings such as *Swamp Gum* (2004) [**PLATE 14**], from the *Beekeepers* series, or *Maculata* (2005) [**PLATE 6**], one of the *Cabin* paintings.

Despite Bush's fluid application of paint and use of hyper-real colors, these paintings are not without restraint. In *Lacque Rose* (2003) [**PLATE 20**] or *Gripped Me Goldly* (2004) [**PLATE 11**], for example, Bush renders the serialized images of apiarist and his boxes with a calculating eye and a steady hand. By merging abstract and figural elements into single works, Bush attempts to collapse the conceptual boundaries that exist between conventional binaries such as organic and man-made, old and new, and colonizer and colonized, or "us" and "them," in order to shift viewers' cultural biases and perspectives.

A sense of ruination, chaos, and unraveling of time and thought are manifest in the humble, dilapidated cabin in *Southeast in the Summer* (2006) [**PLATE 1**], and in the fragments of architectural elements hovering aimlessly in *Bimblebox Poplar* (2005) [**PLATE 3**] and *Citriodora* (2005) [**PLATE 4**]. The strange silence that permeates these pictures is juxtaposed by loud, clashing colors, concealing the alienation and melancholic emptiness that seems to lie just below their surfaces. The presence of the landscape, once a dominant leitmotif that symbolized cultural identity and the "mastery" of European academic tradition, has been emptied of denotative meaning, allowing us to bask in the saturated hues of the unknown and let our imaginations run wild.

[1] All biographical information, unless otherwise noted, is courtesy of the artist's conversation with the author, 2006.

plates

PLATE 1

Southeast in the Summer, 2006

Oil and enamel on linen

72 x 72 inches

Courtesy of Sutton Gallery, Melbourne, Australia

Collection of Ken & Lisa Fehily, Melbourne, Australia

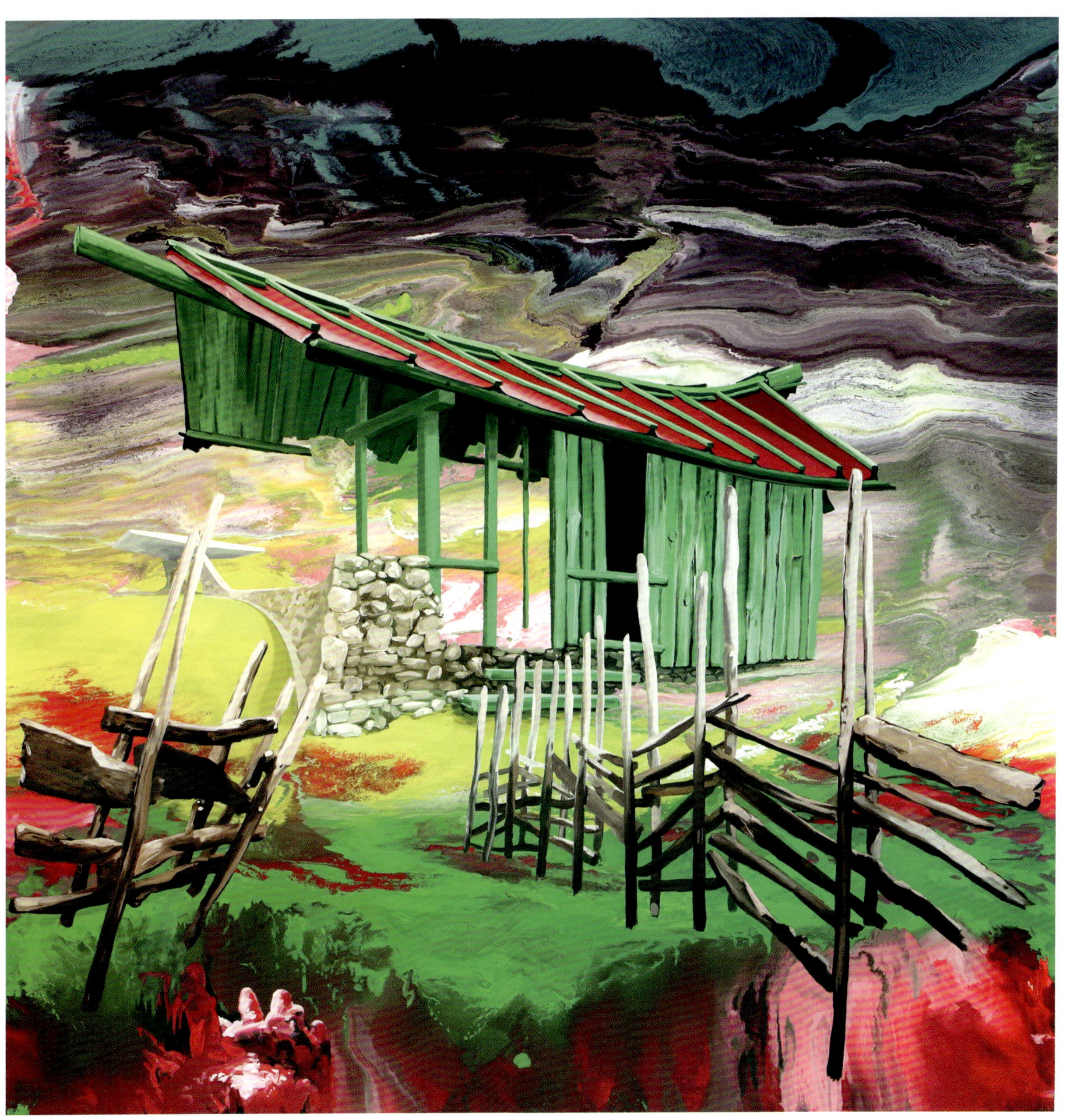

PLATE 2

Yanchep, 2006

Oil and enamel on linen

72 x 72 inches

Courtesy of Goff + Rosenthal, New York, NY

Collection of Gary & Marilyn Hellinger, Greenwich, CT

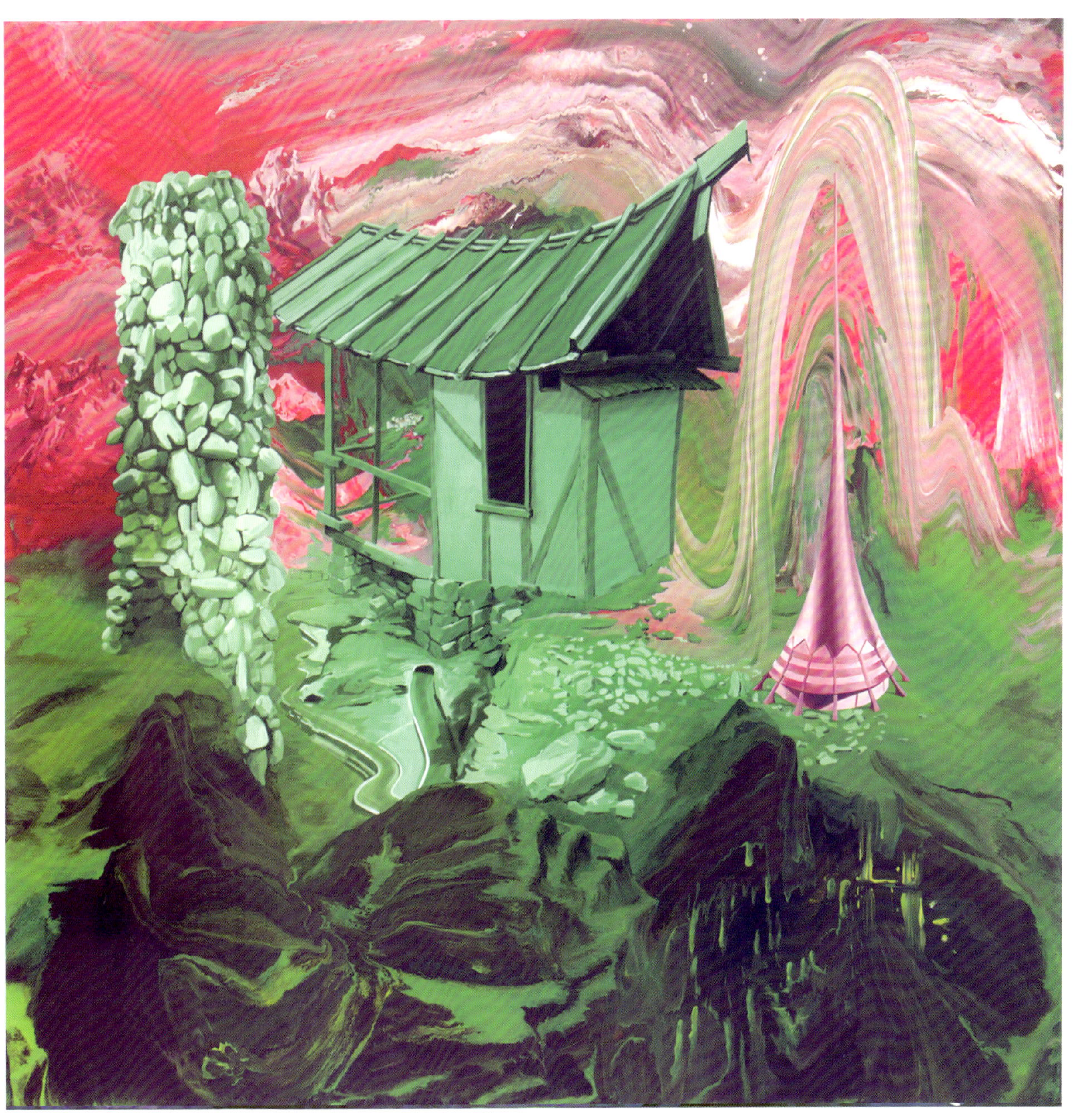

Bimblebox Poplar, 2005

Oil and enamel on linen

66 x 78 Inches

Courtesy of Sutton Gallery, Melbourne, Australia

Collection of John & Irene Sutton, Melbourne, Australia

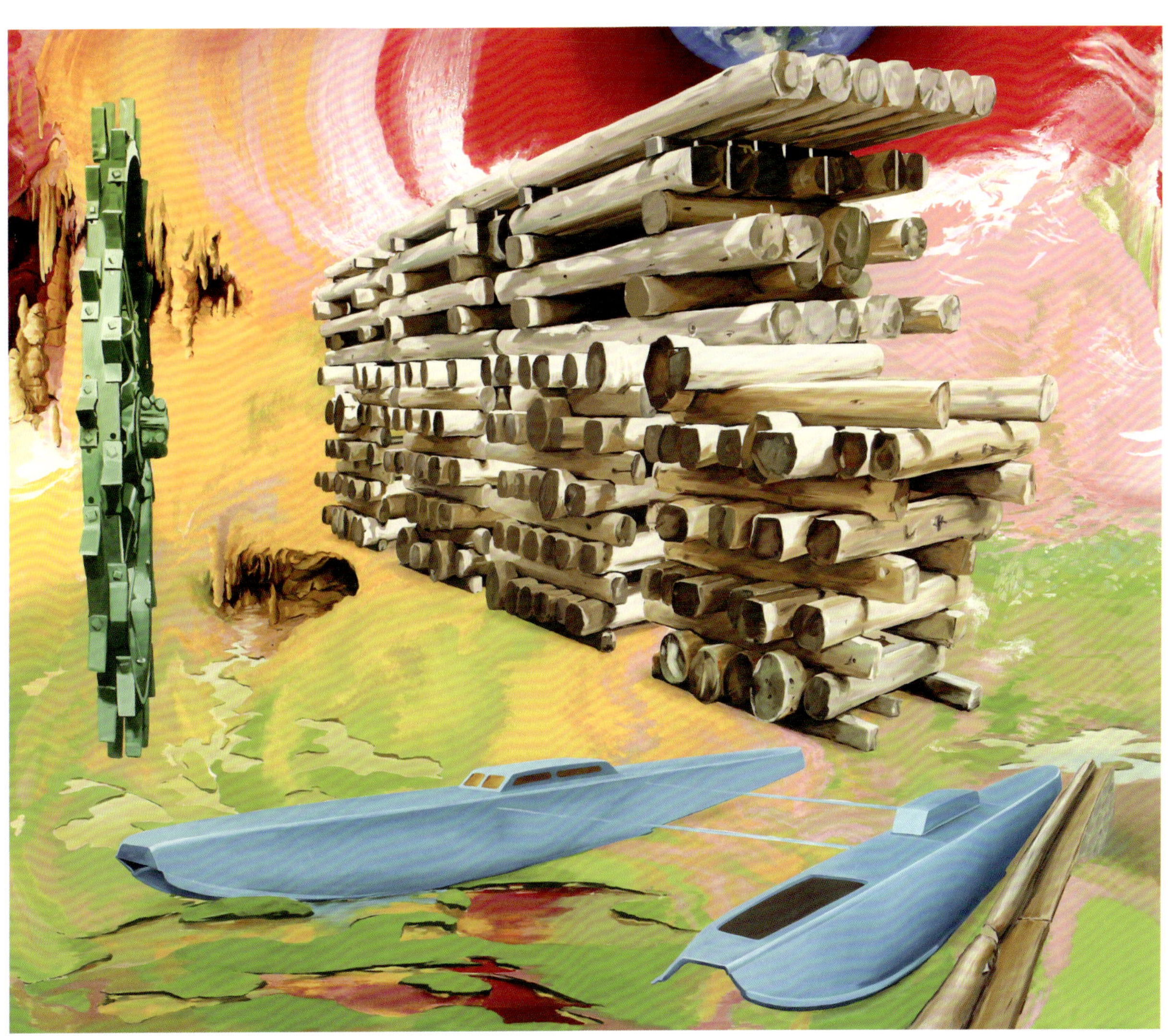

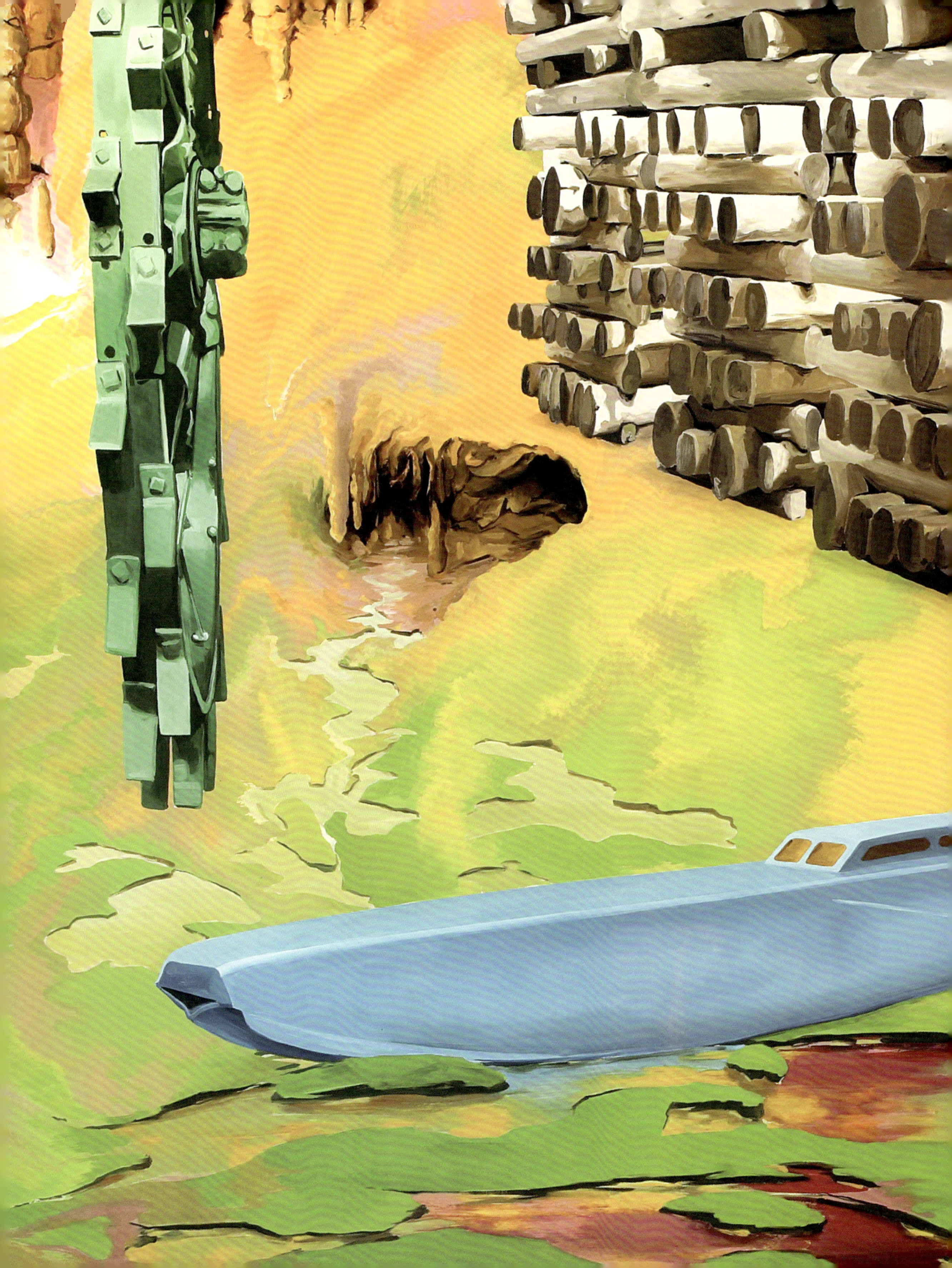

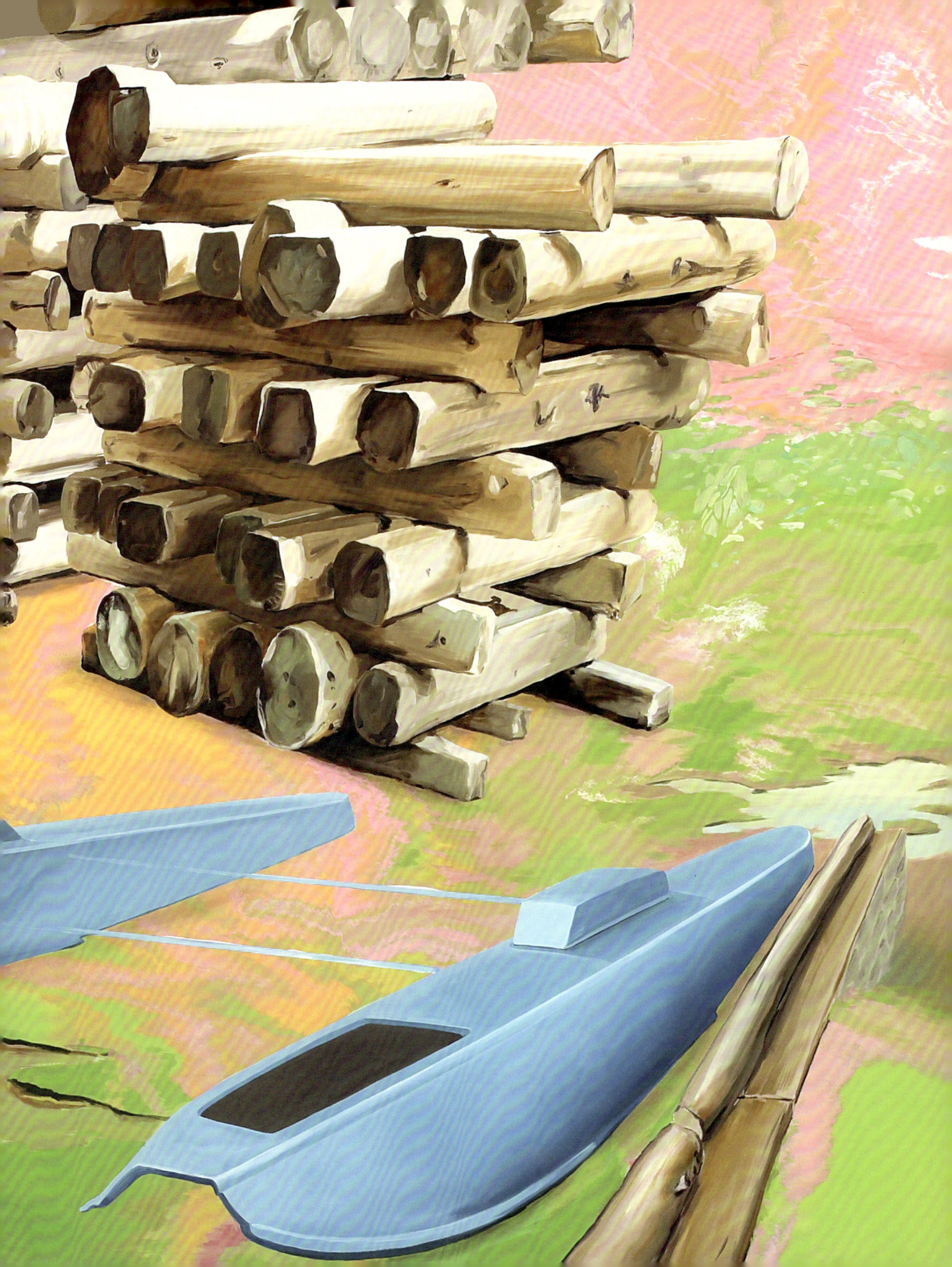

PLATE 4

Citriodora, 2005

Oil and enamel on linen

72 x 72 inches

Courtesy of Sutton Gallery, Melbourne, Australia

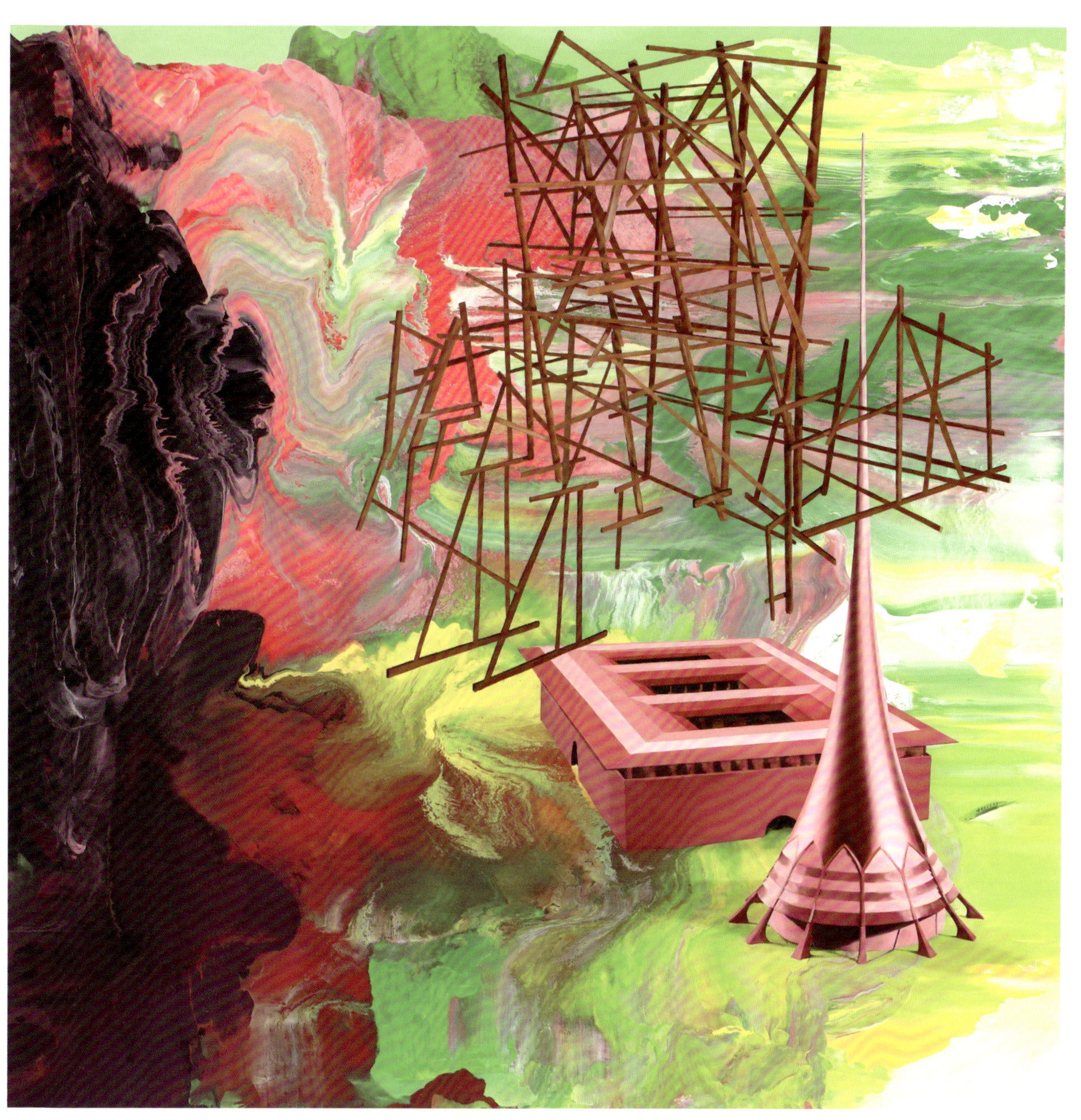

PLATE 5

Ericifolia, 2005

Oil and enamel on linen

38 x 38 inches

Courtesy of Goff + Rosenthal, New York, NY

Collection of HG Rosen

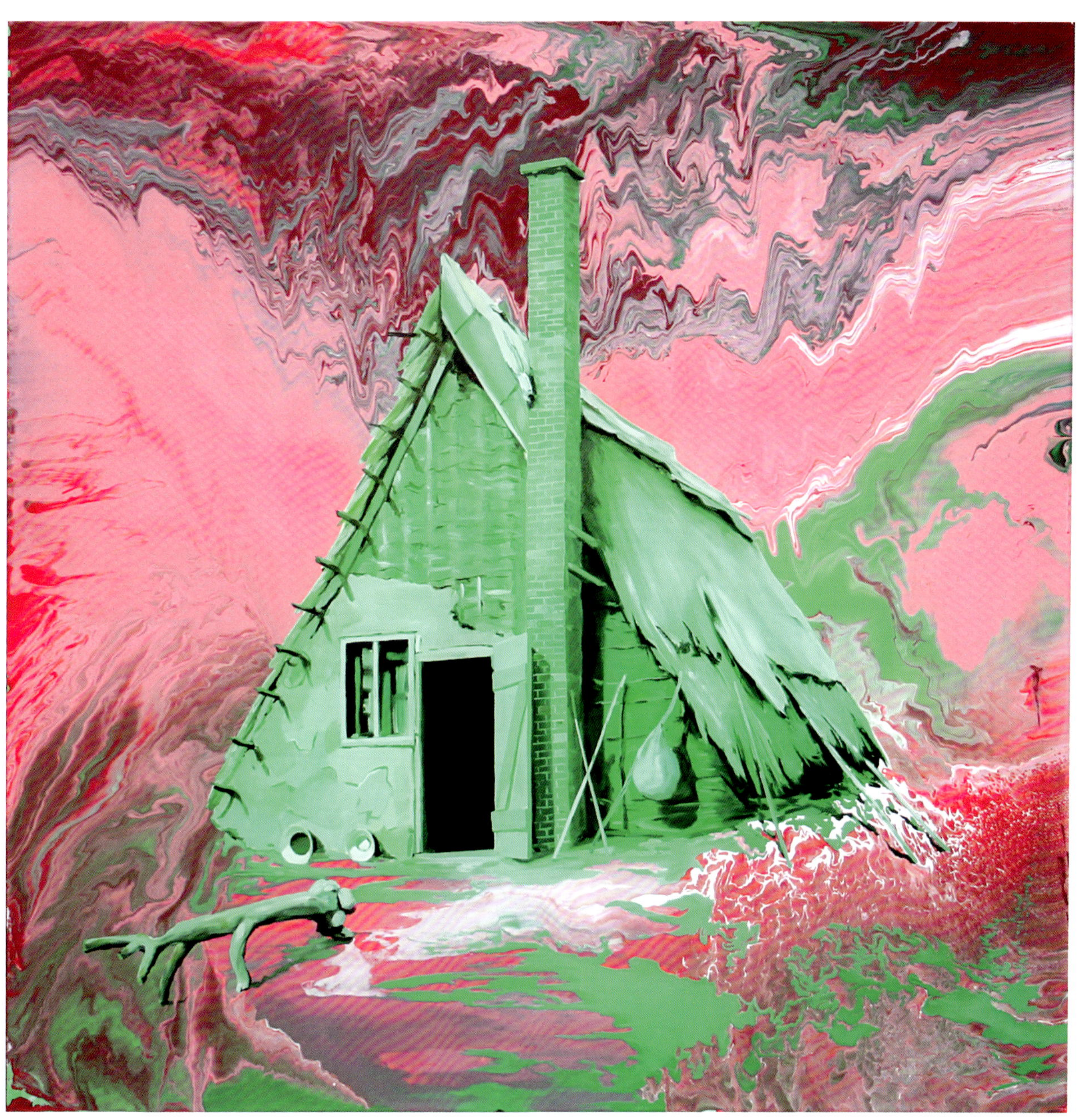

PLATE 6

Maculata, 2005

Oil and enamel on linen

72 x 72 inches

Collection of Bobbi & Stephen Rosenthal

Not in exhibition

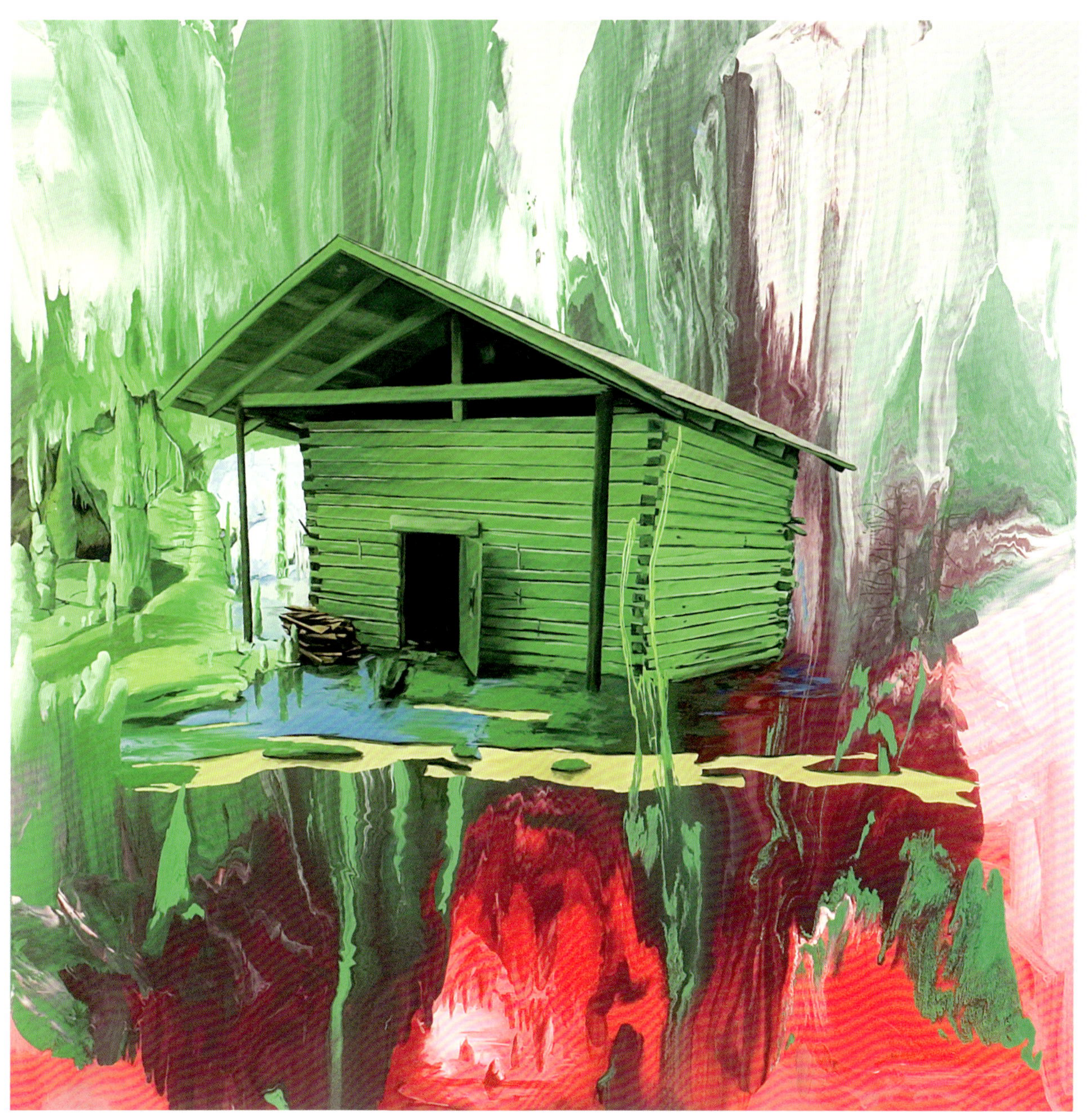

PLATE 7

Viminalis, 2005

Oil and enamel on linen

72 x 72 inches

Courtesy of Goff + Rosenthal, New York, NY

Collection of Saam Farhang

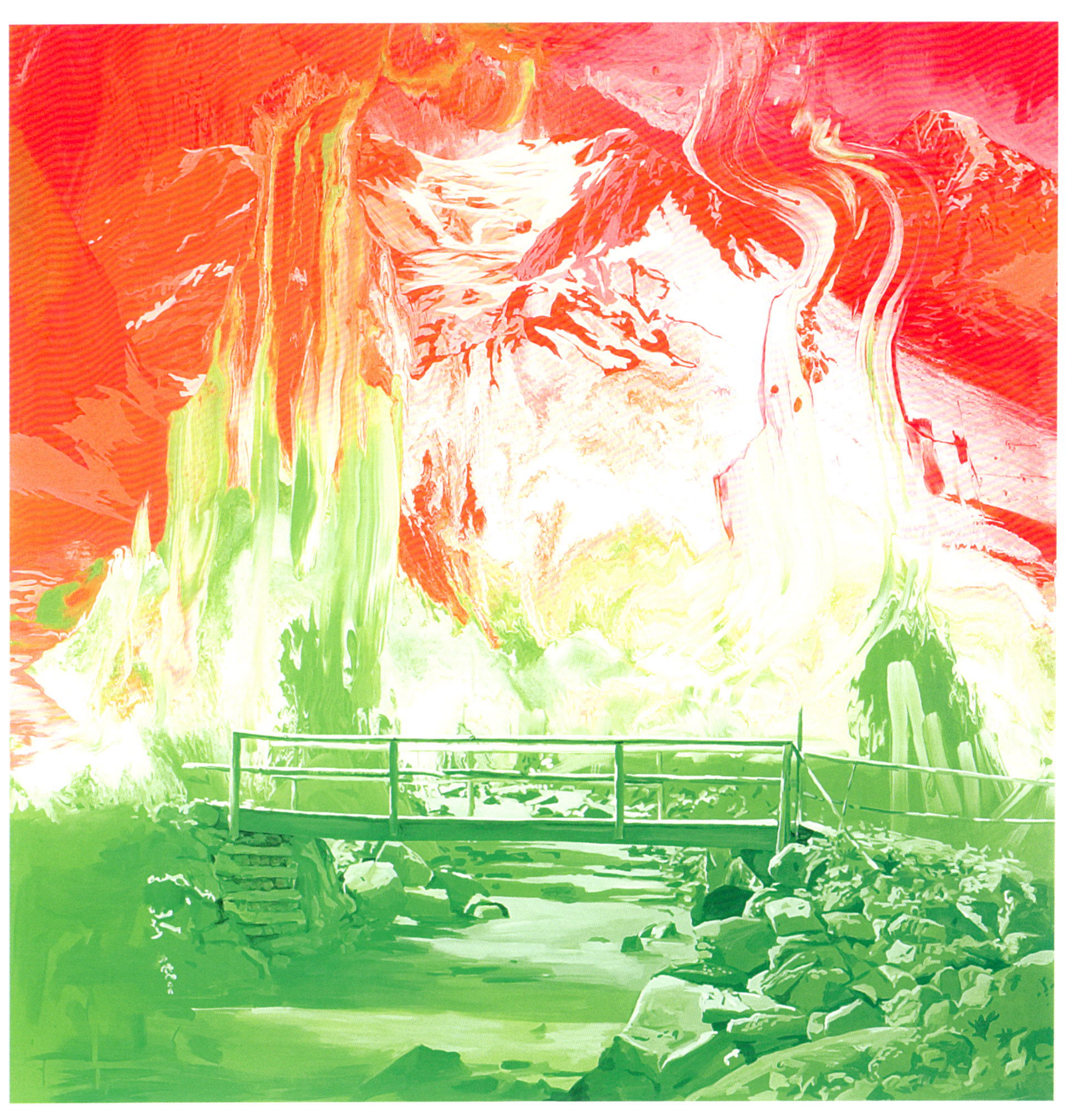

Sure Nuff Yes I Do, 2004

Oil and enamel on linen

72 x 72 inches

Courtesy of Sutton Gallery, Melbourne, Australia

Private collection, Melbourne, Australia

Not in exhibition

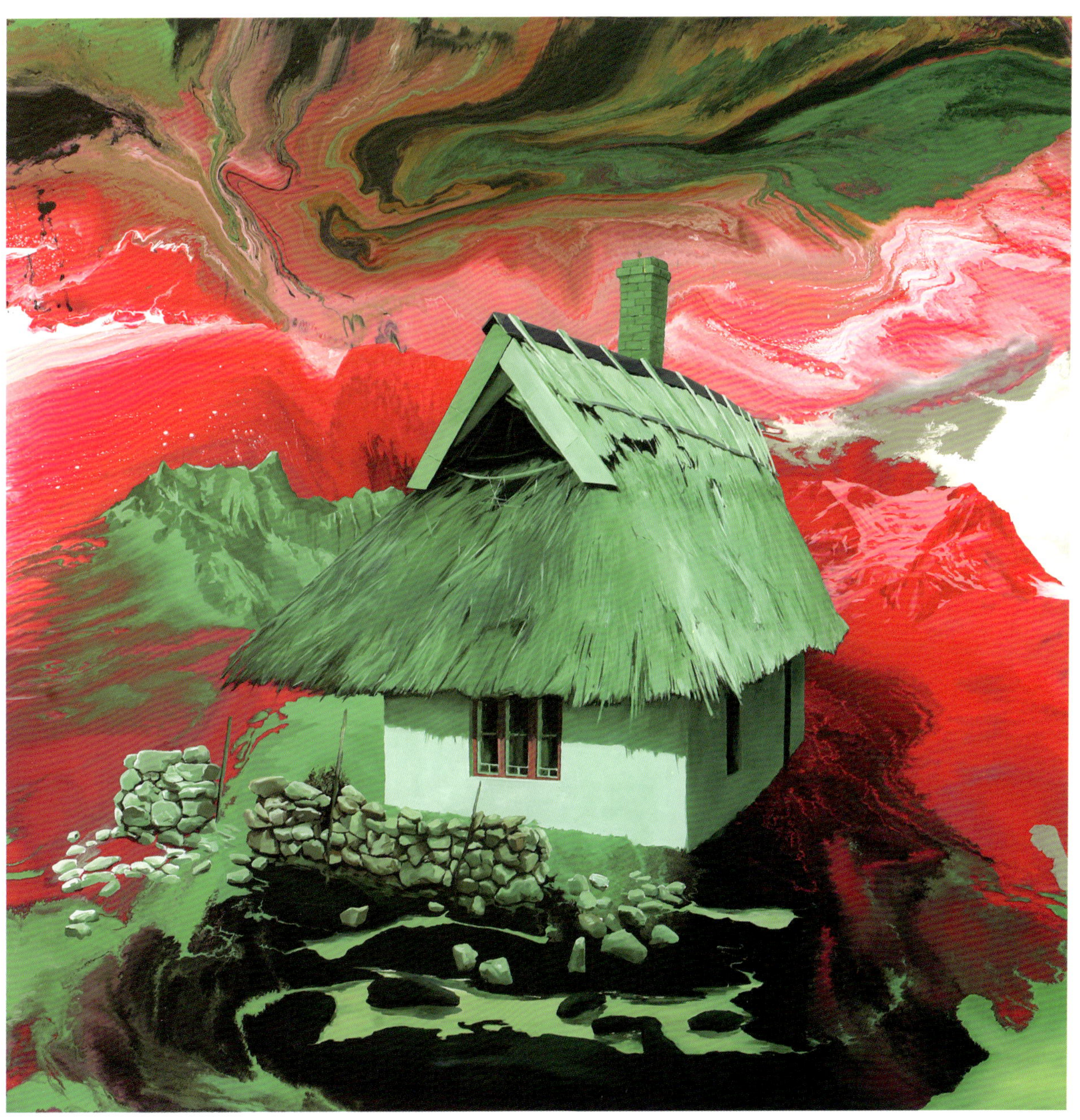

PLATE 9

Brighten My Northern Sky, 2004

Oil and enamel on linen

38 x 30 inches

Courtesy of Sutton Gallery, Melbourne, Australia

Private collection, Melbourne, Australia

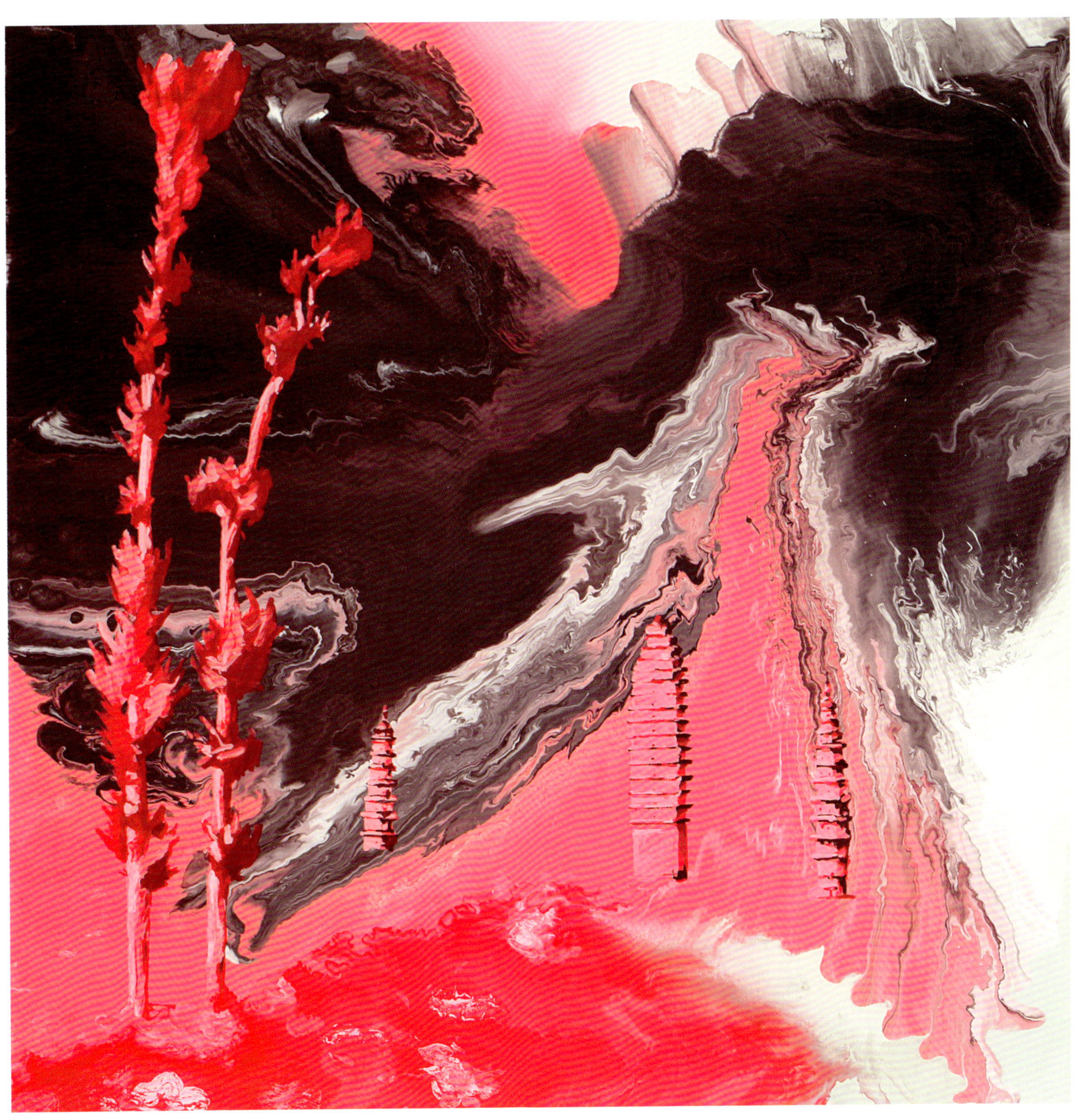

PLATE 10

Gelderland, 2004

Oil on linen

78 x 92 inches

Courtesy of Sutton Gallery, Melbourne, Australia

Not in exhibition

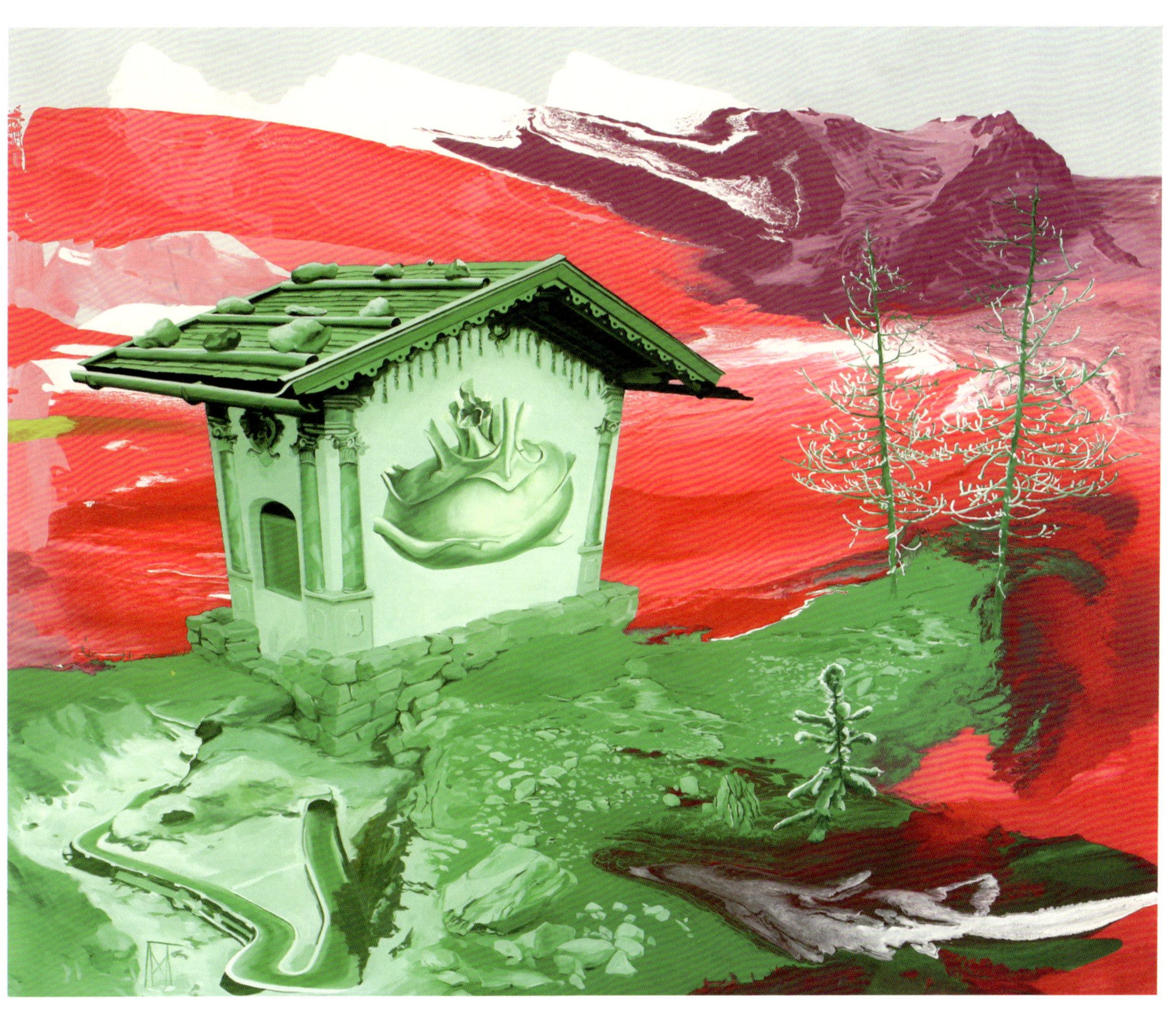

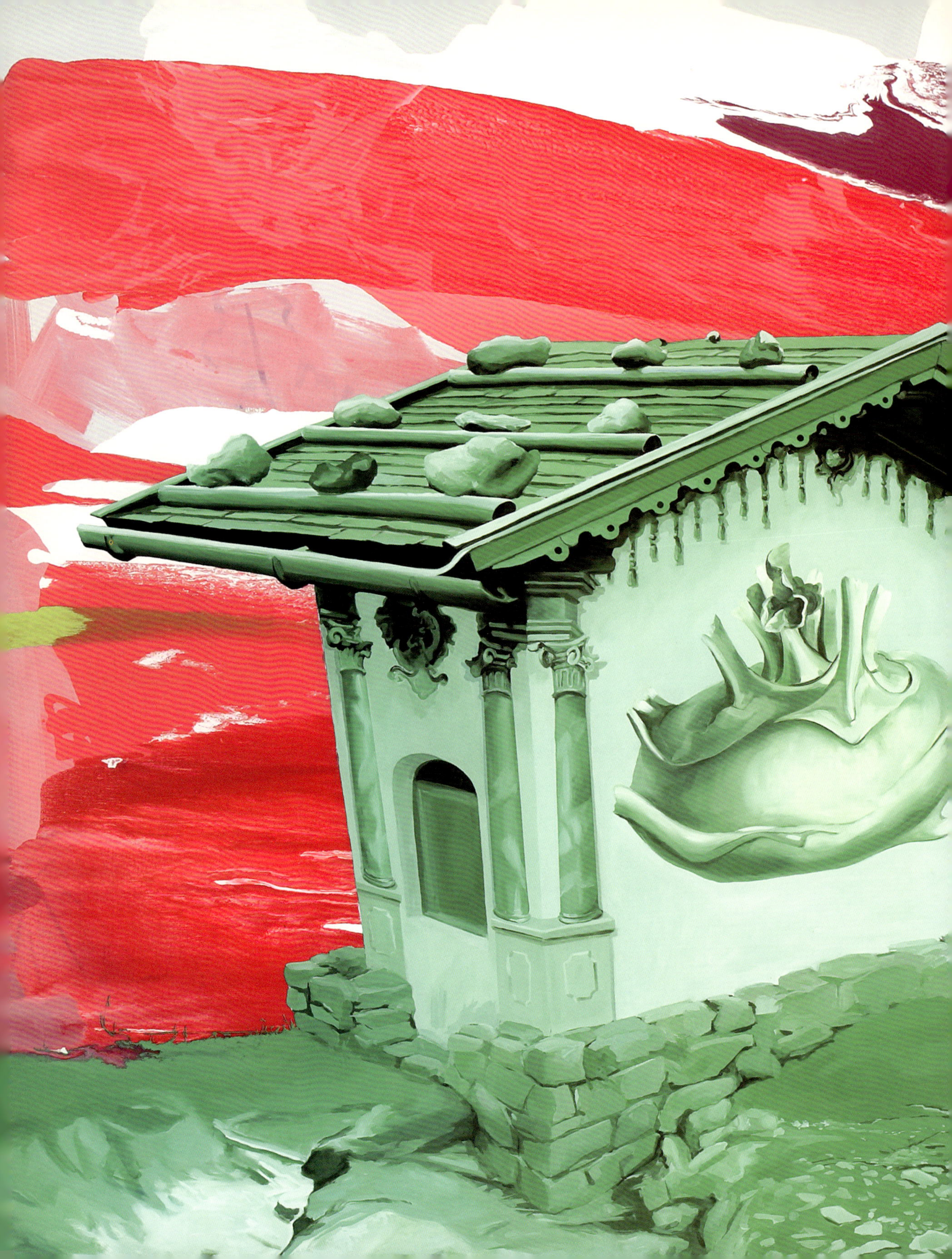

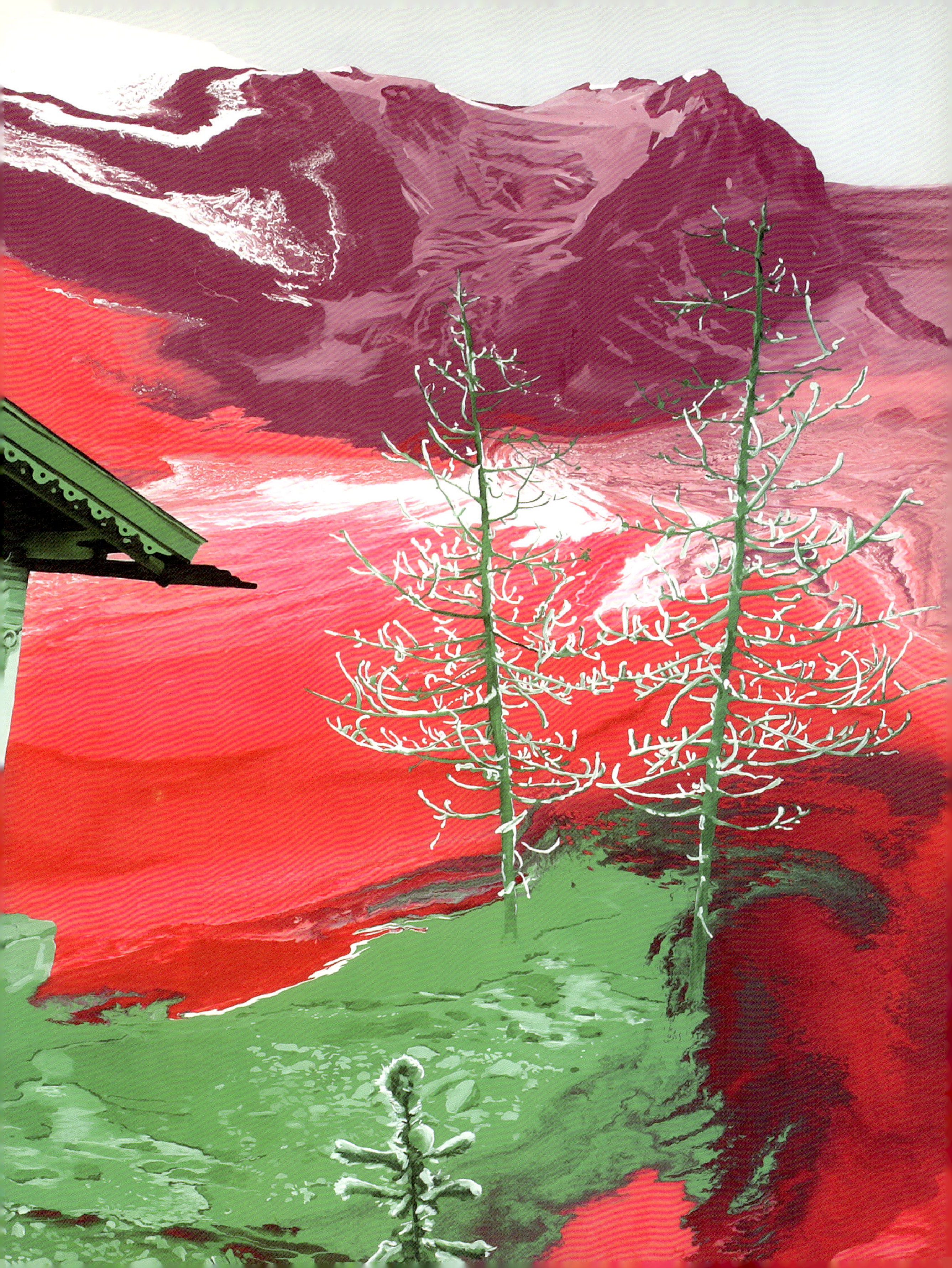

PLATE 11

Gripped Me Goldly, 2004

Oil and enamel on linen

72 x 72 inches

Courtesy of Sutton Gallery, Melbourne, Australia

Private collection, Melbourne, Australia

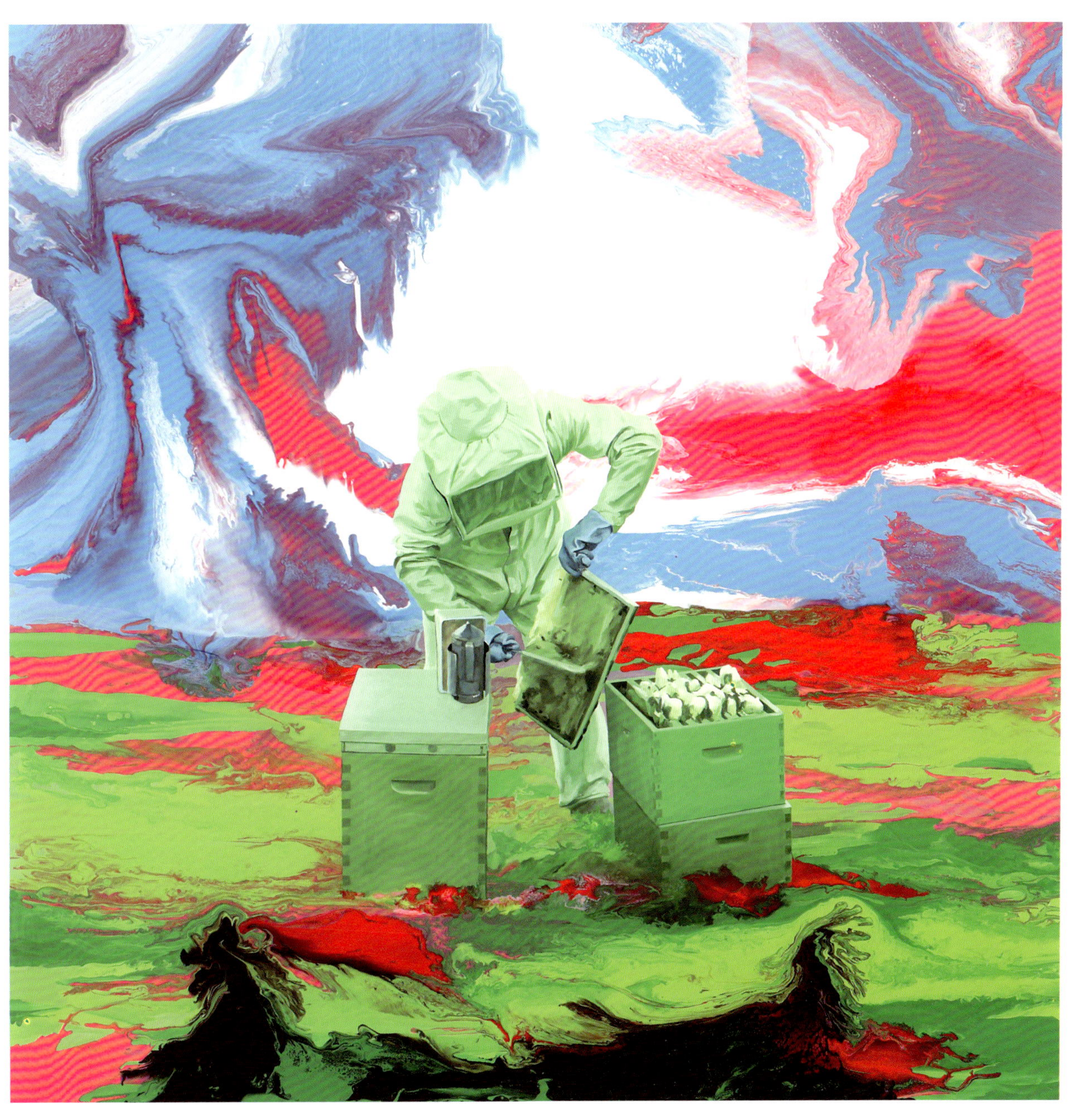

PLATE 12

Jean, 2004

Oil and enamel on linen

13.8 x 15 inches

Courtesy of Sutton Gallery, Melbourne, Australia

Private collection, Melbourne, Australia

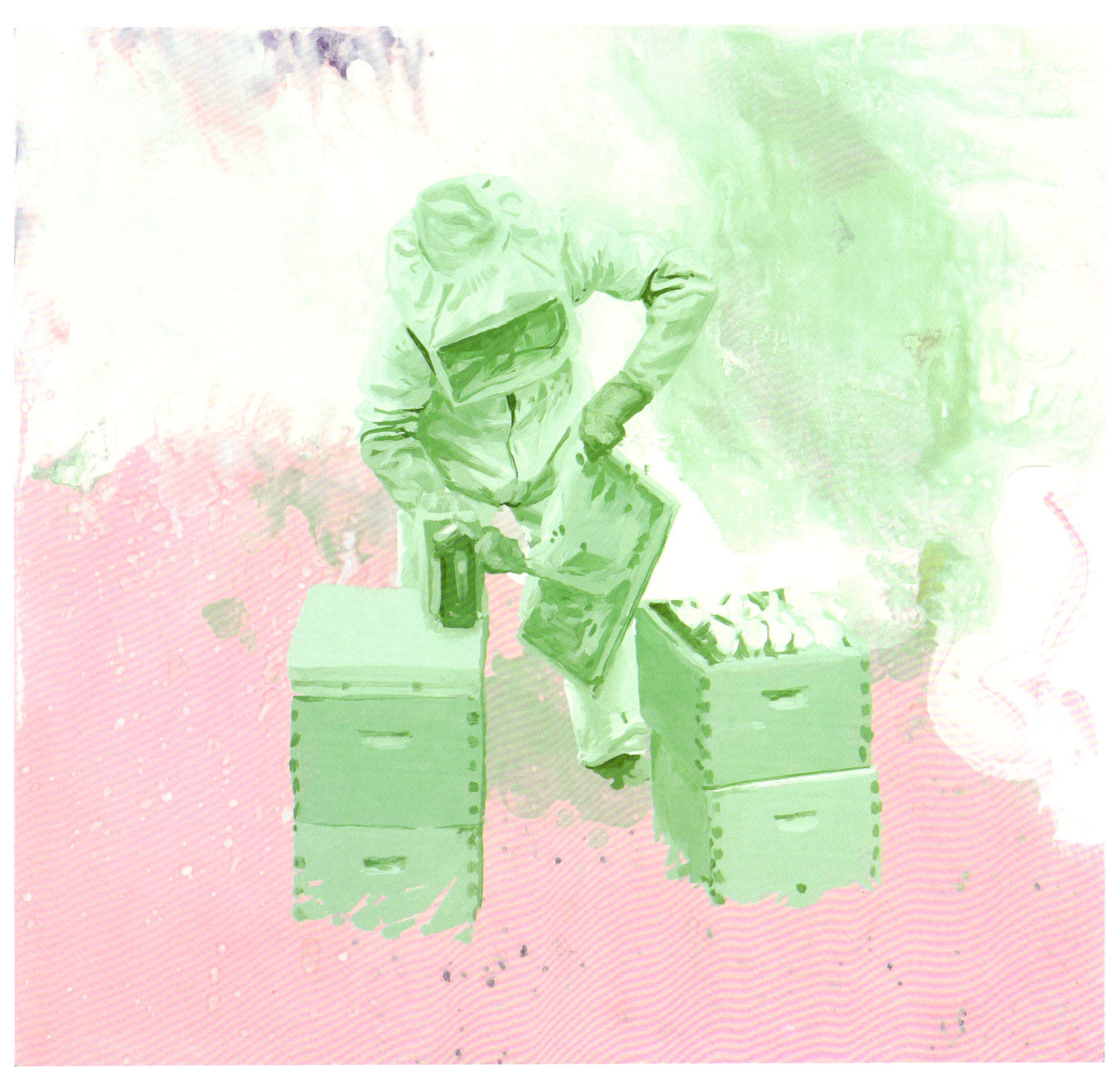

PLATE 13

Lauterbrunnental, 2004

Oil and enamel on linen

38 x 72 inches

Courtesy of Sutton Gallery, Melbourne, Australia

Not in exhibition

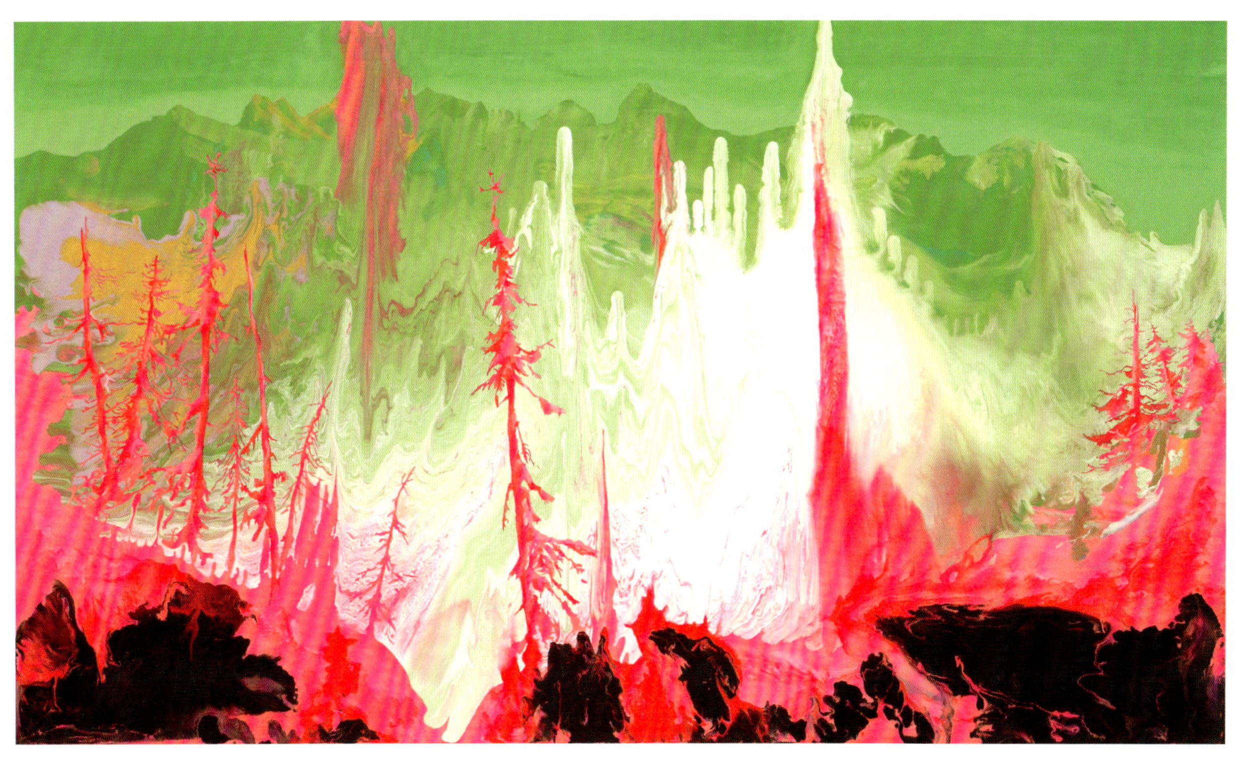

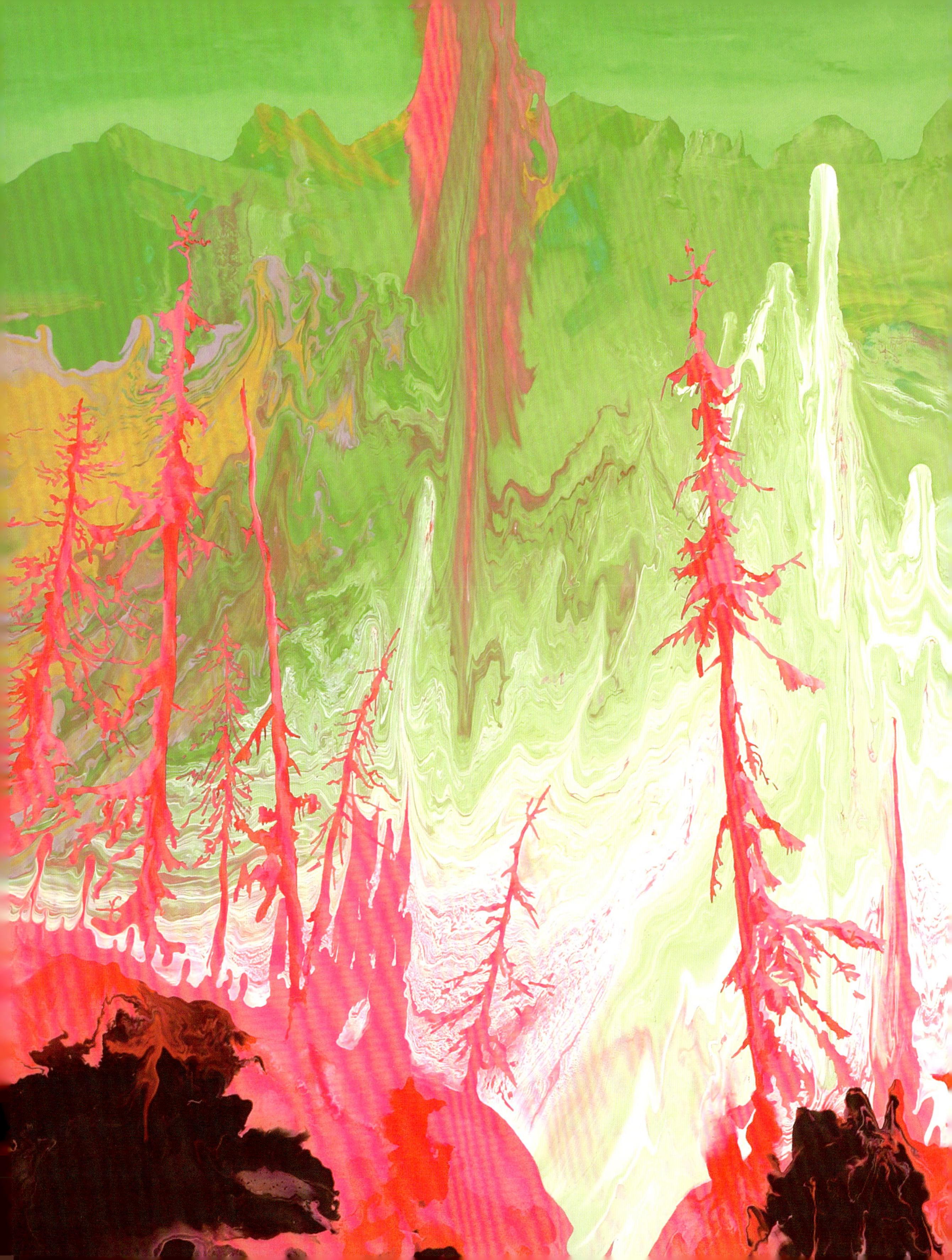

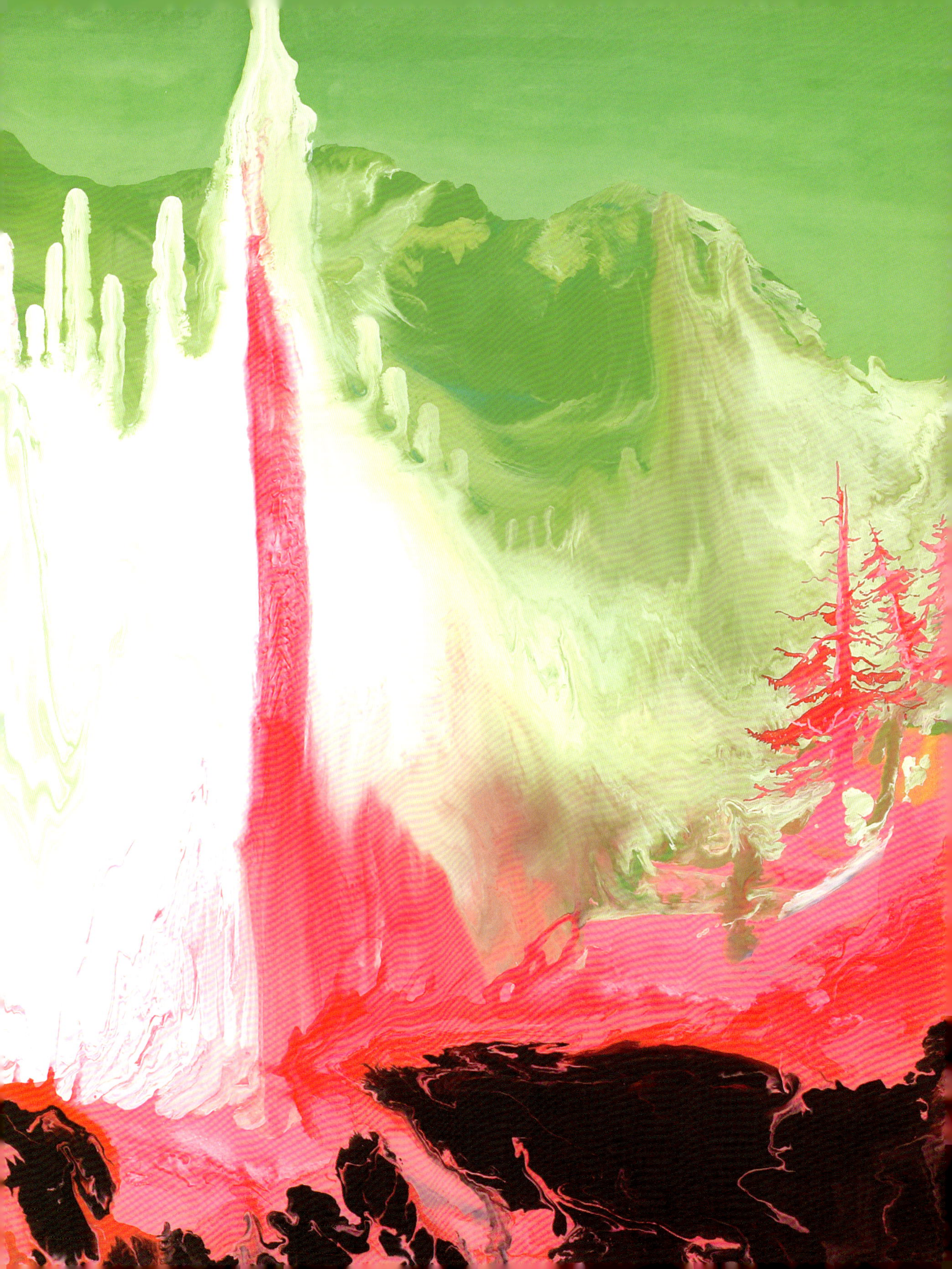

PLATE 14

Swamp Gum, 2004

Oil and enamel on linen

72 x 72 inches

Collection of John L. Stewart, New York, NY

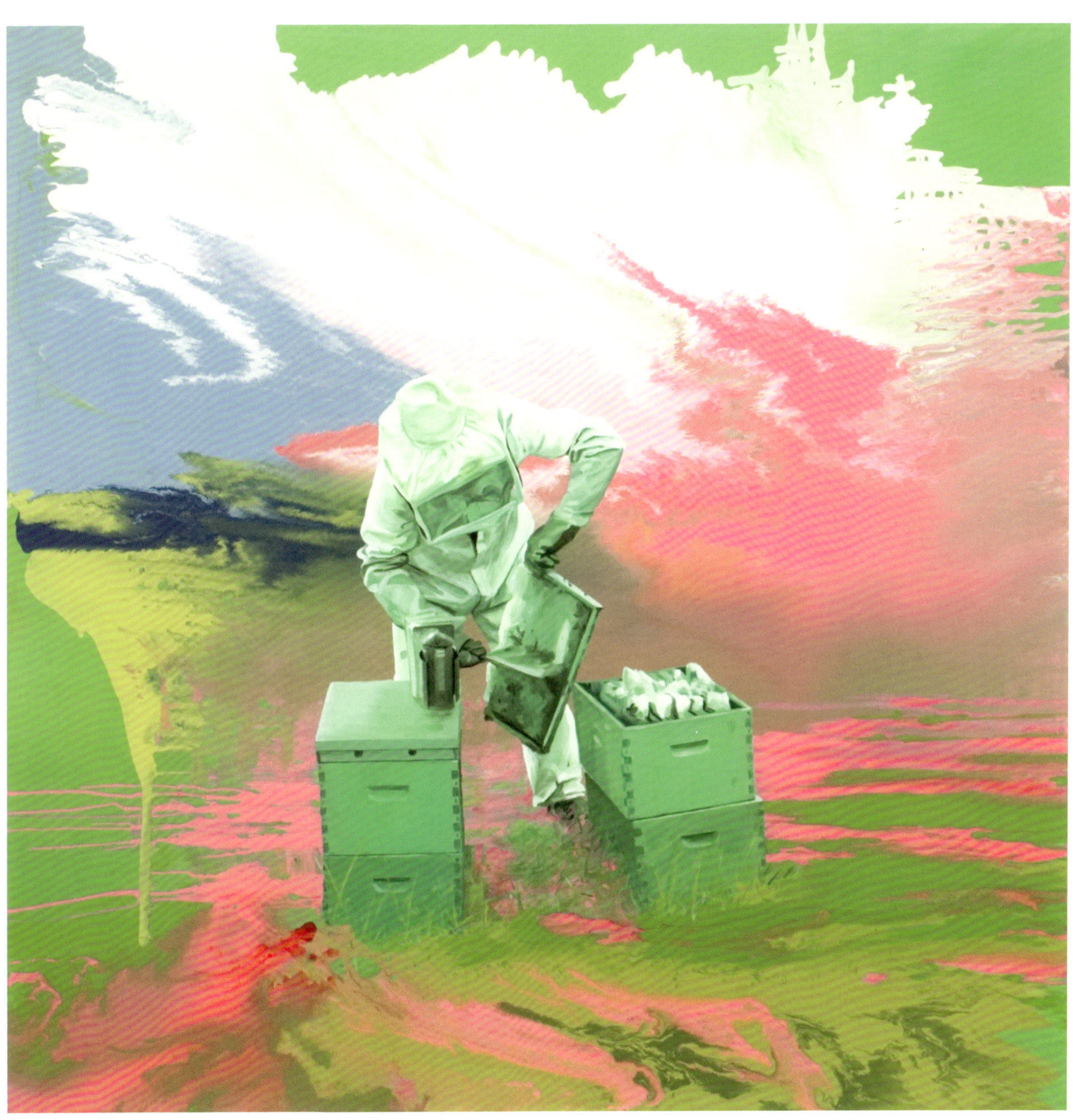

PLATE 15

Tallow Wood, 2004

Oil and enamel on linen

72 x 72 inches

Courtesy of Goff + Rosenthal, New York, NY

Collection of David Teplitzky

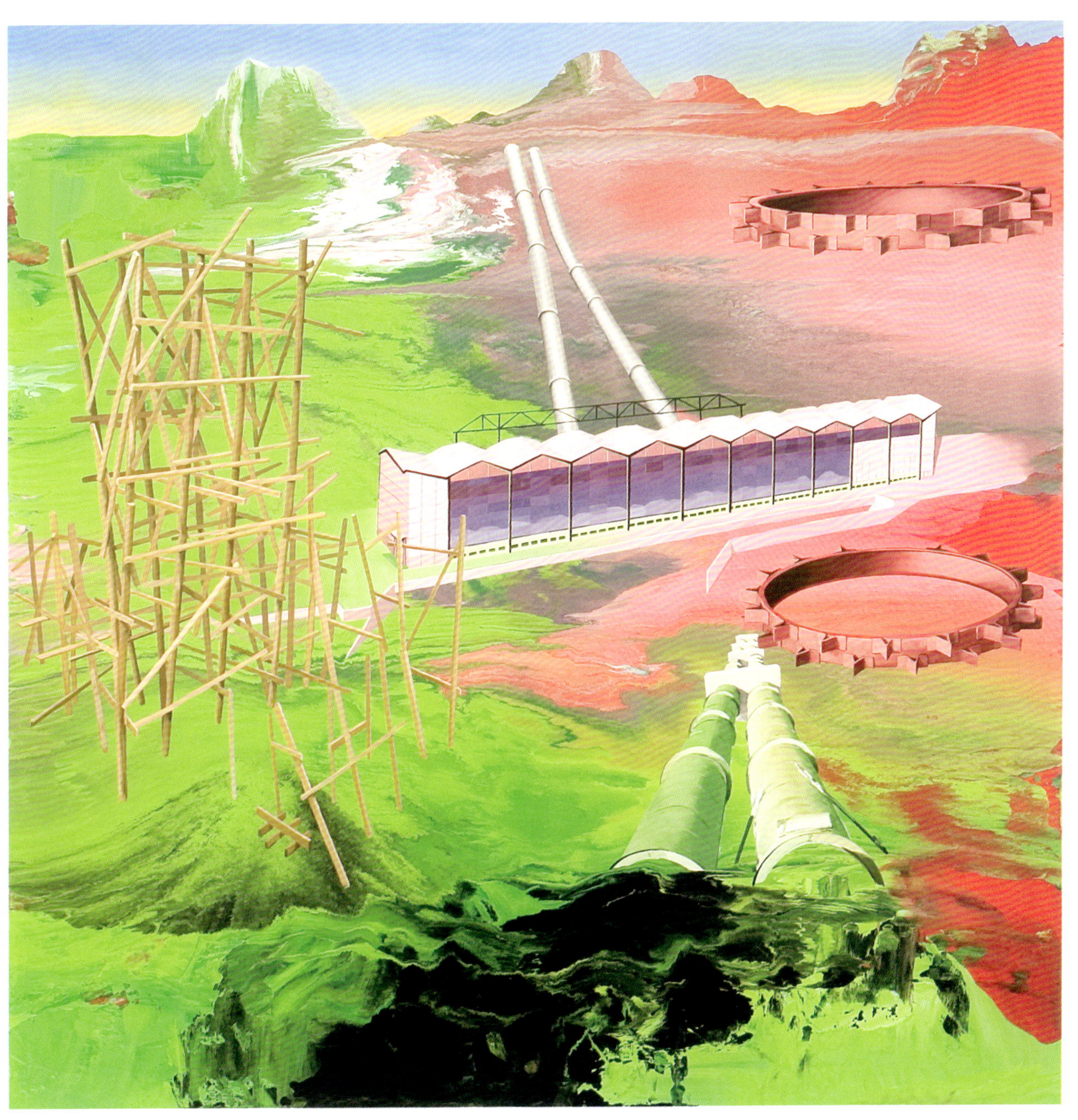

PLATE 16

Vert Or, 2004

Oil and enamel on linen

22 x 26 inches

Courtesy of Sutton Gallery, Melbourne, Australia

Private collection, Melbourne, Australia

Vert de Sevres, 2004

Oil and enamel on linen

72 x 72 inches

Collection of John L. Stewart, New York, NY

Not pictured

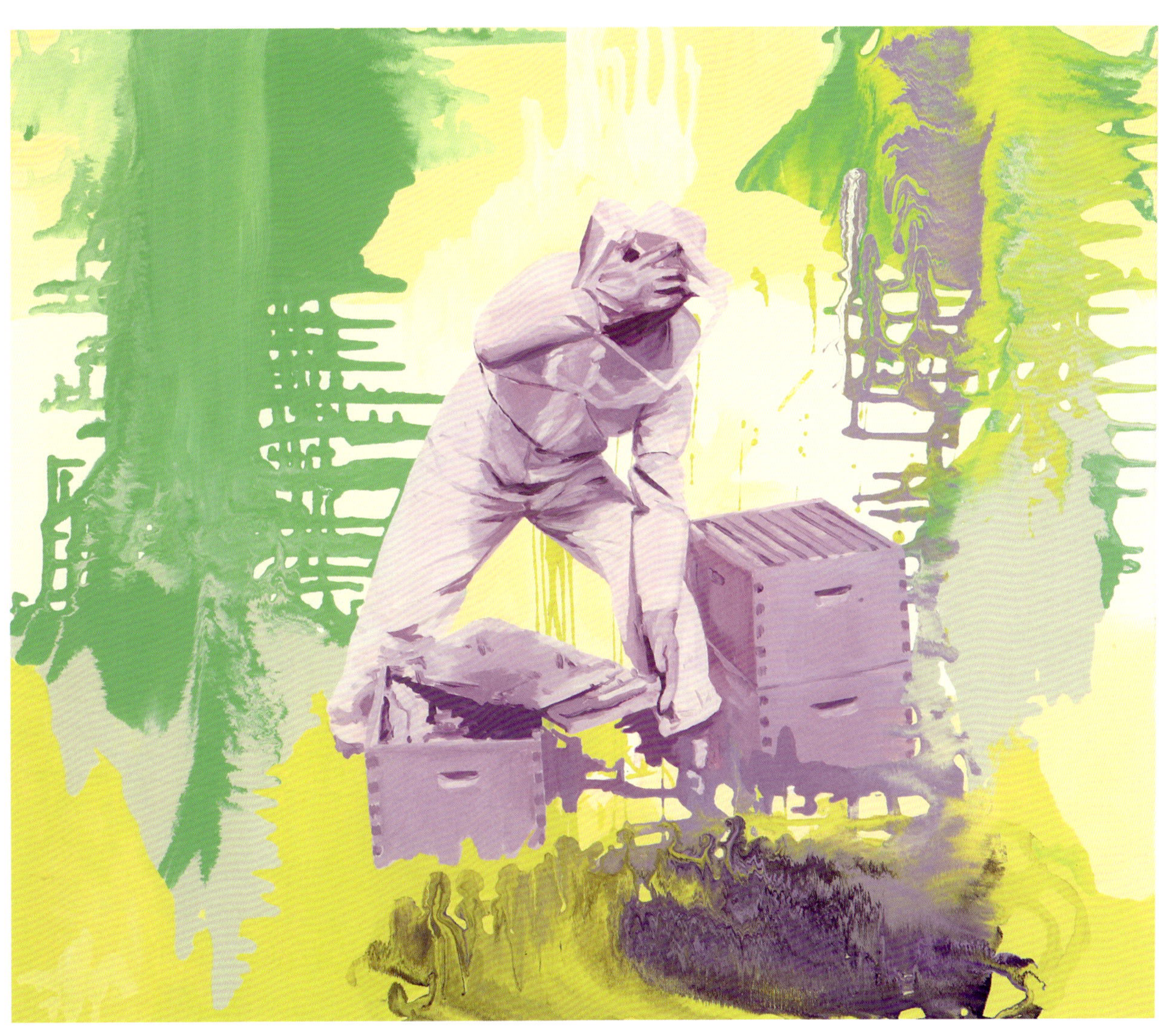

PLATE 17

Big Eye Beams, 2003

Oil on linen

78 x 92 inches

Courtesy of Sutton Gallery, Melbourne, Australia

Collection of Stephanie & Julian Grose, Adelaide, Australia

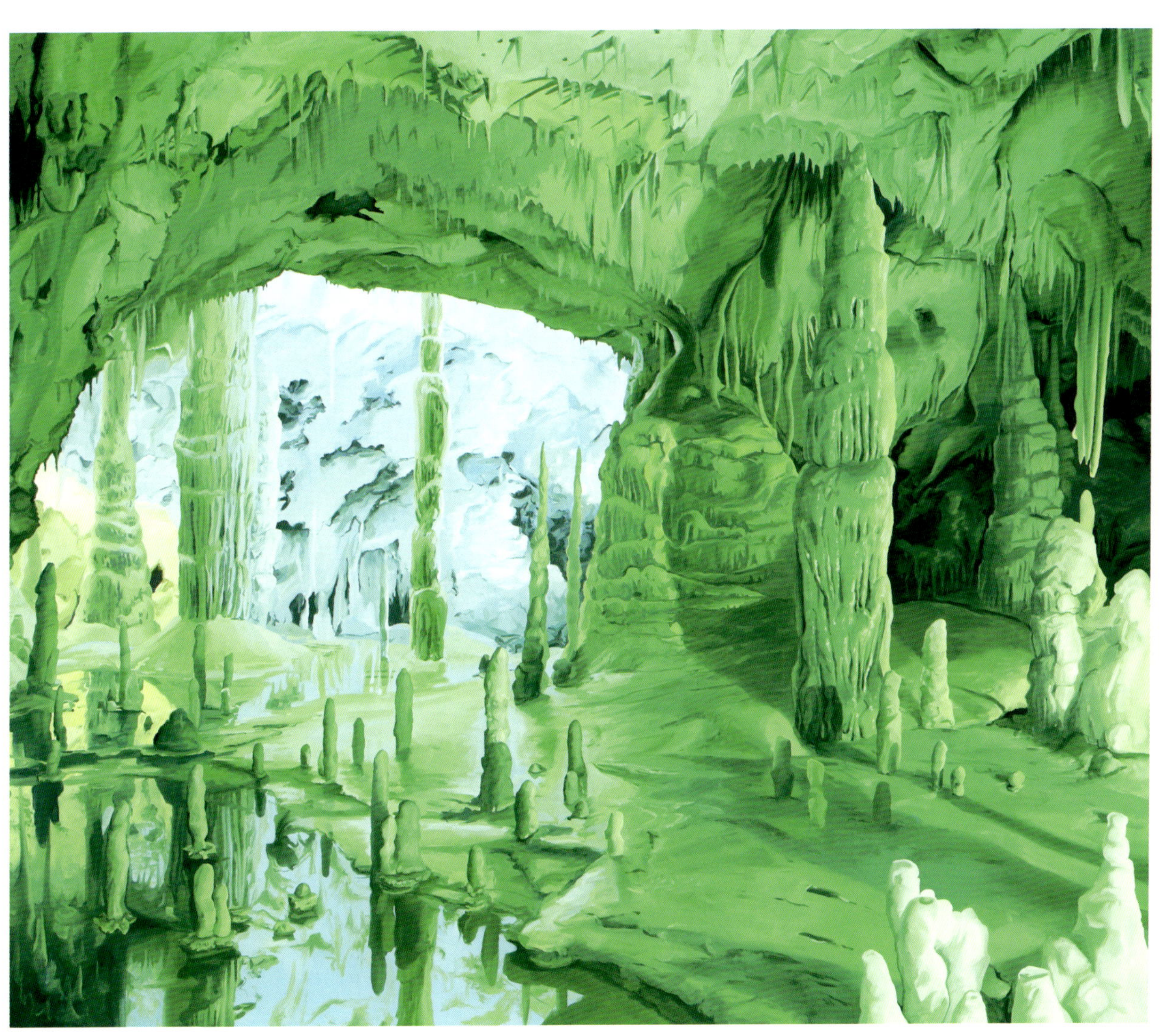

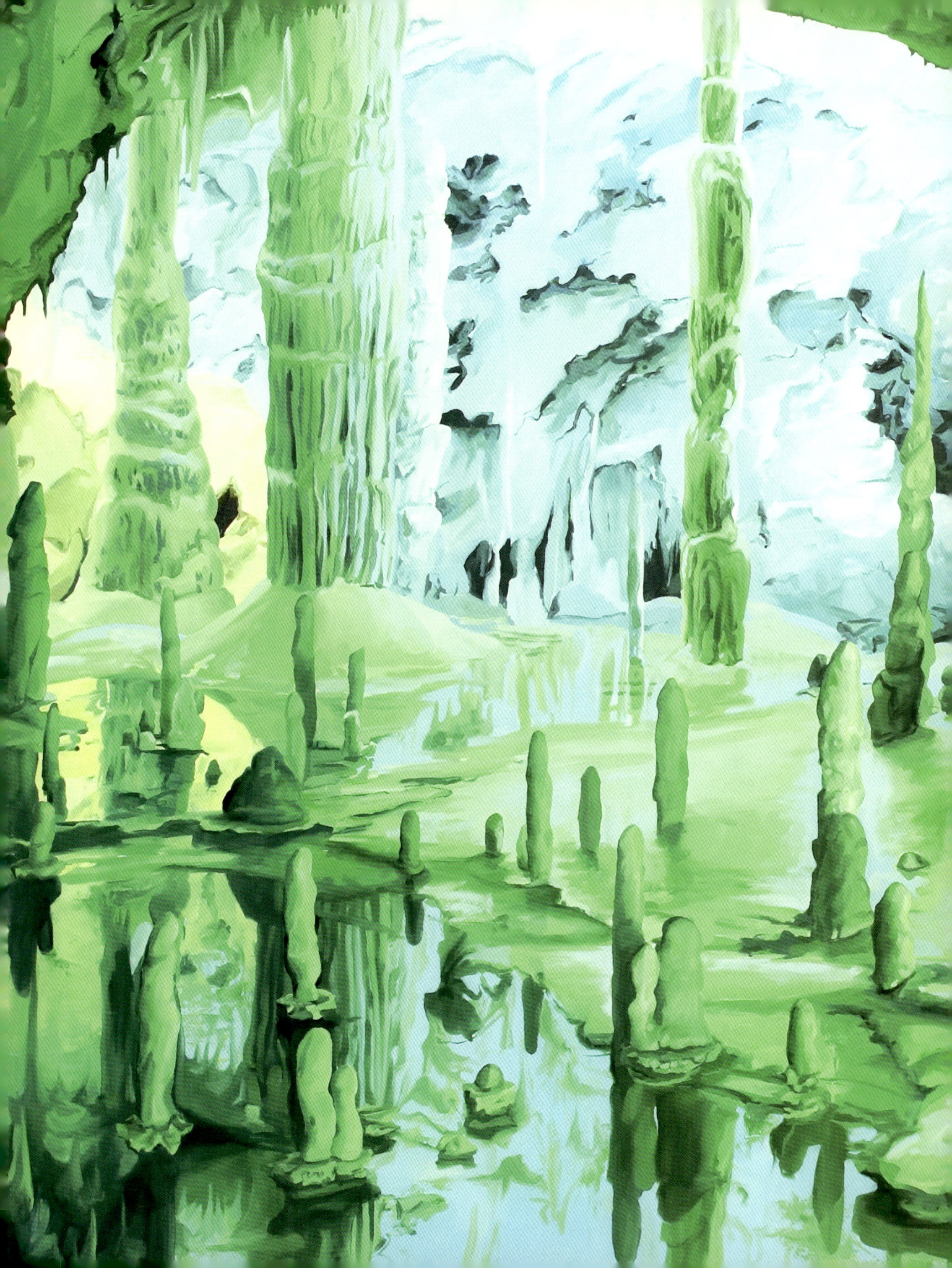

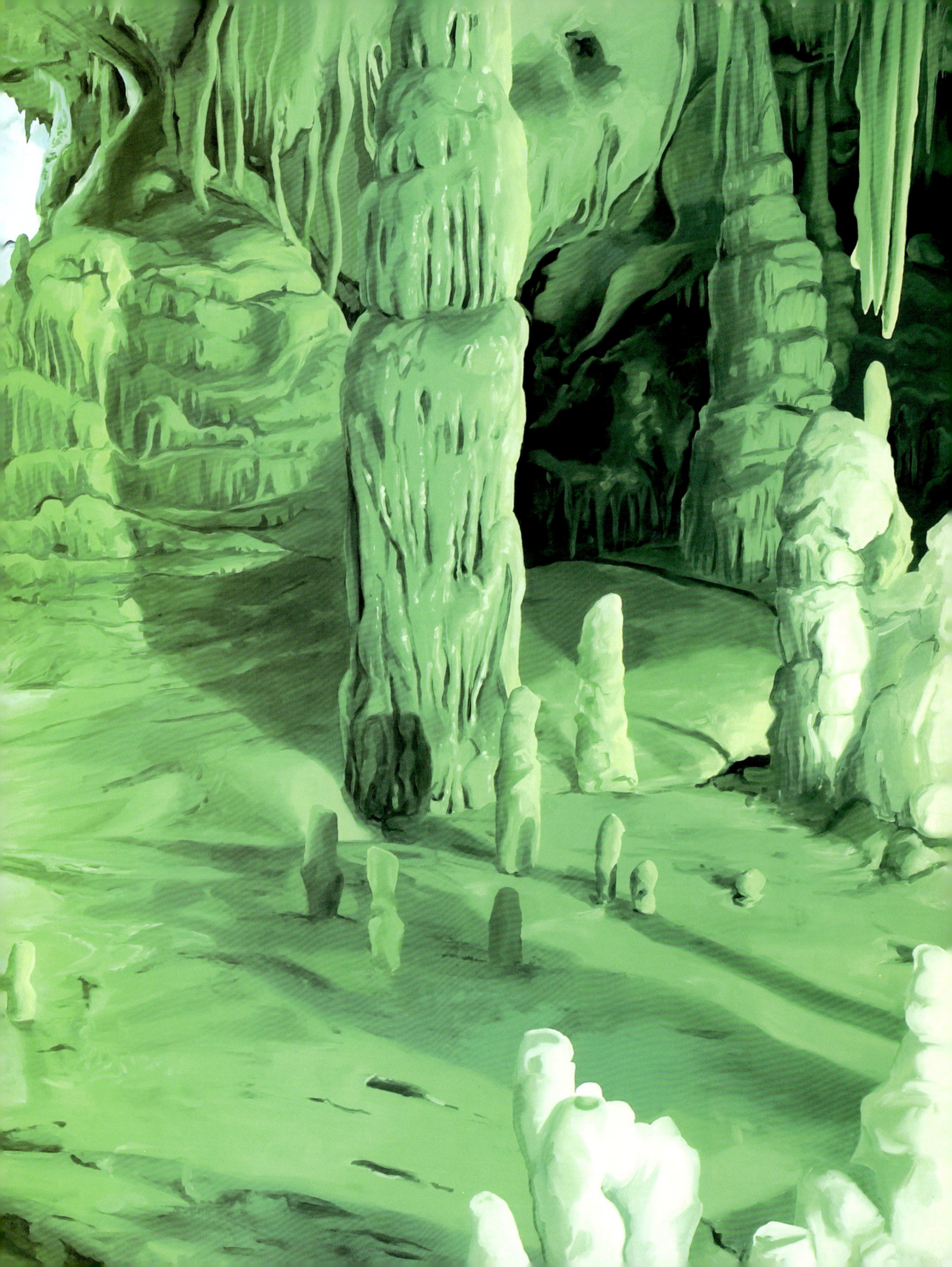

PLATE 18

I Have Come to the Creek, 2003

Oil and enamel on linen

70 x 110 inches

Courtesy of Sutton Gallery, Melbourne, Australia

Collection of Anne & Bernard Shafer, Melbourne, Australia

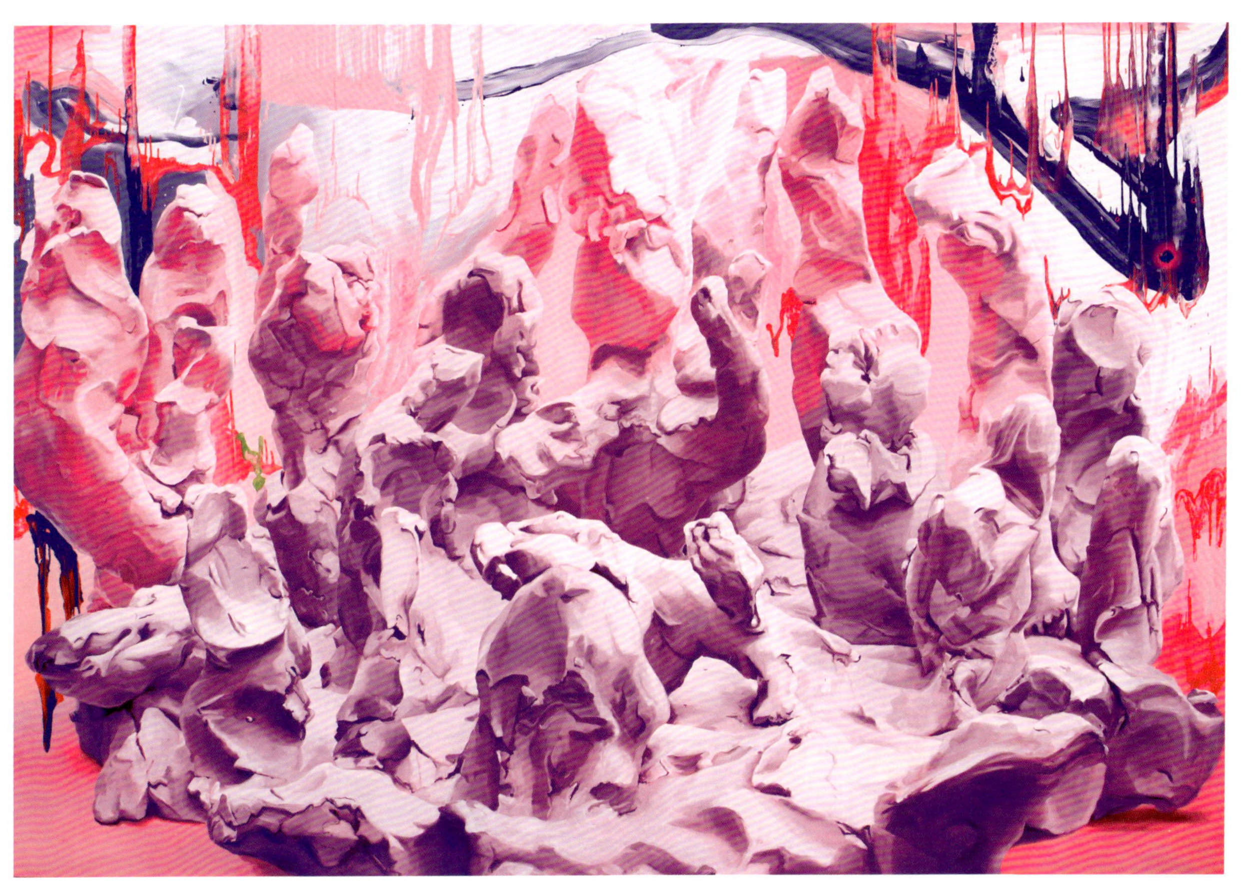

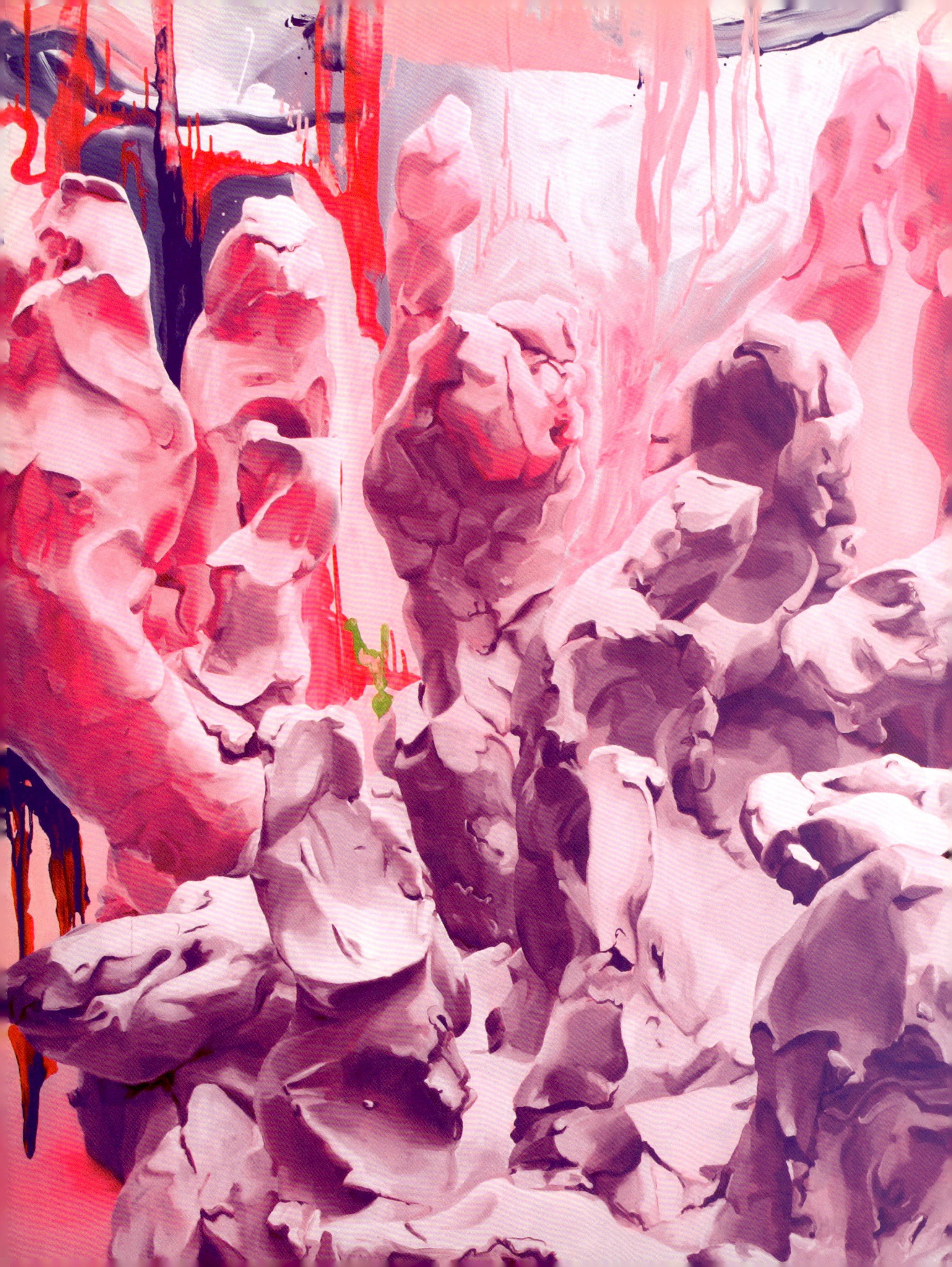

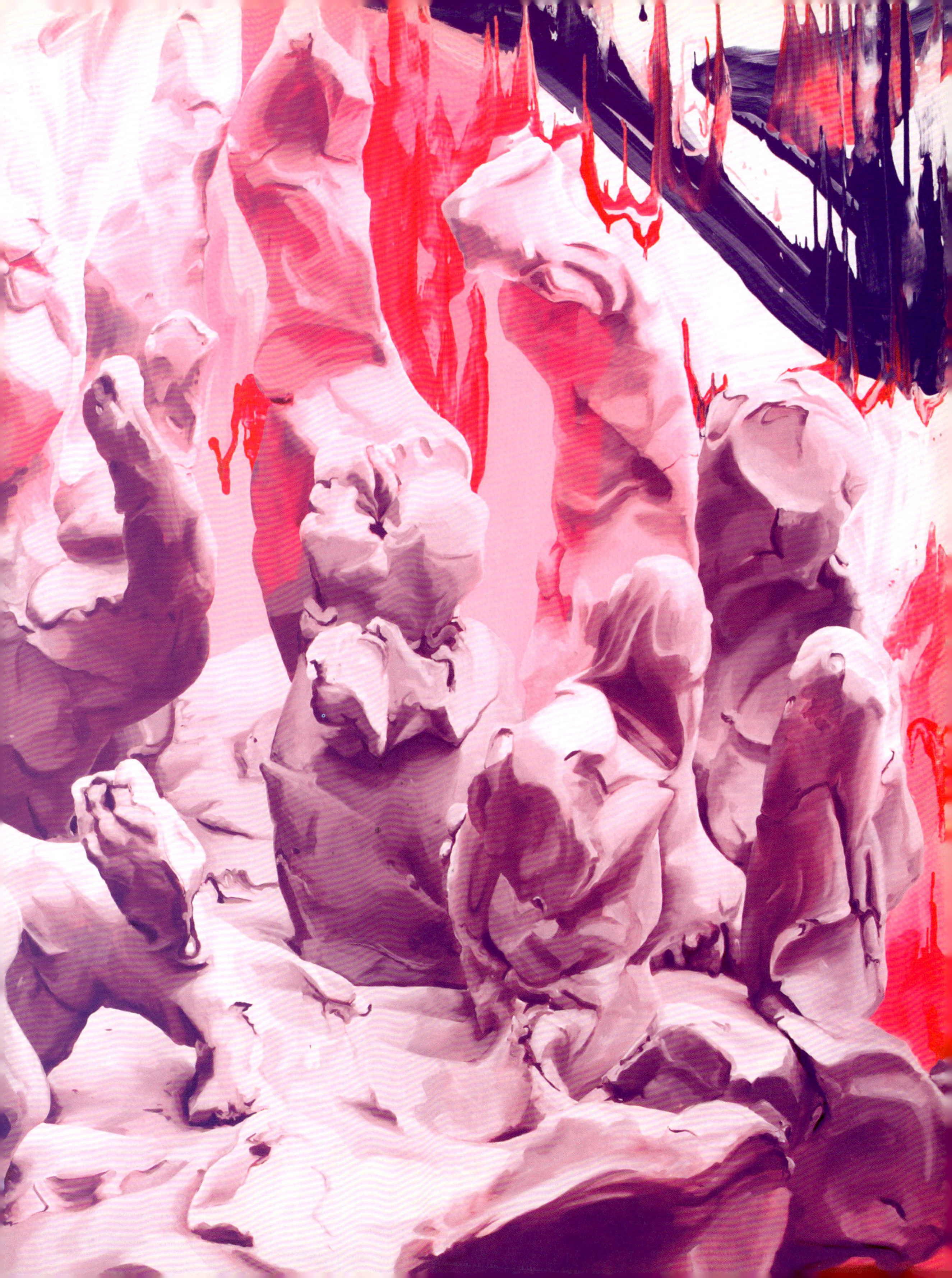

PLATE 19

Jaune de Nickel, 2003

Oil and enamel on linen

22 x 26 inches

Courtesy of Sutton Gallery, Melbourne, Australia

Private colllection, Melbourne, Australia

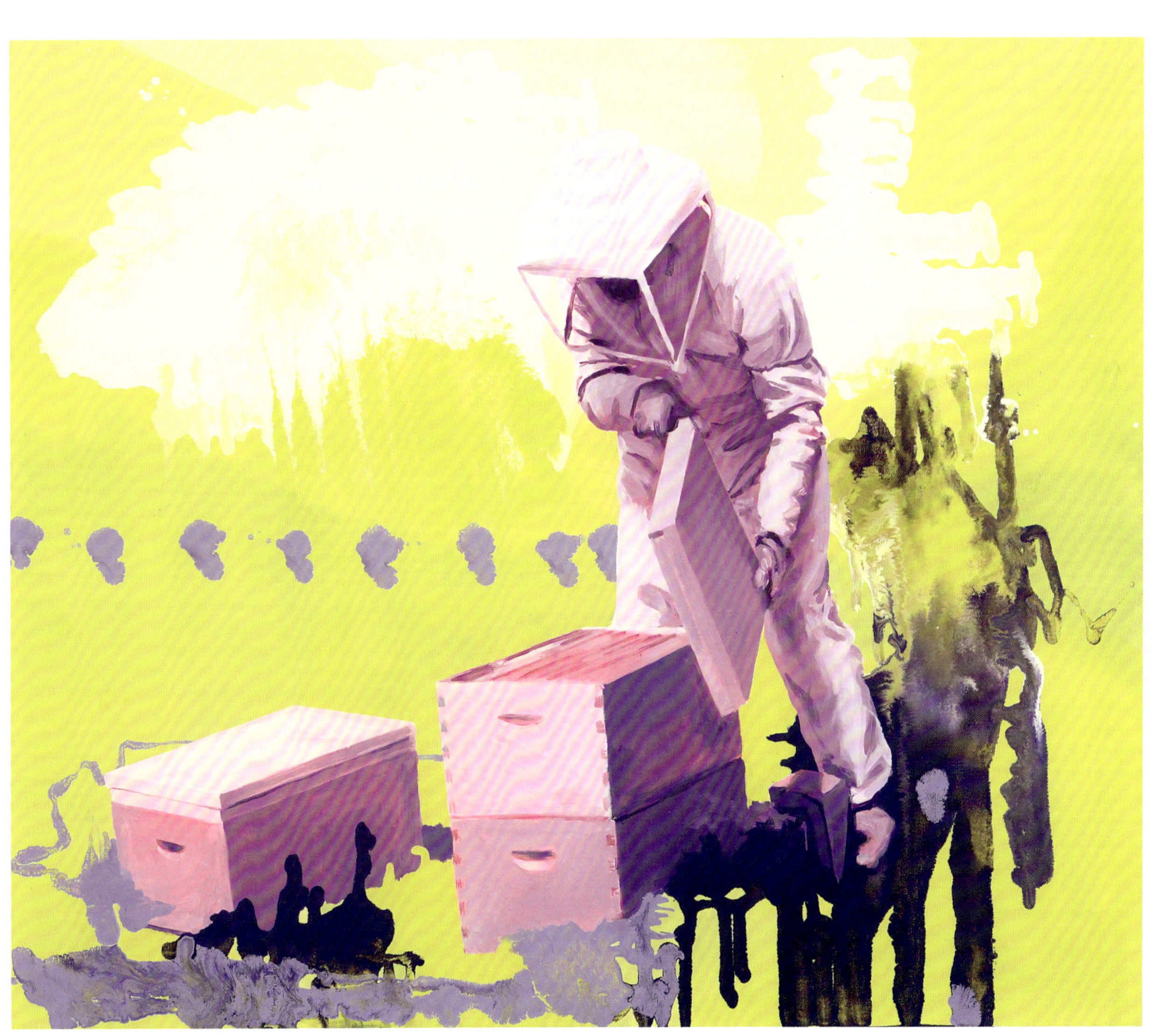

Lacque Rose, 2003

Oil and enamel on linen

20 x 20 inches

Courtesy of Sutton Gallery, Melbourne, Australia

Collection of Annabel & Rupert Myer, Melbourne, Australia

Lacque Rose Fonce, 2003

Oil and enamel on linen

38 x 38 inches

Collection of Jeff & Karen Block, San Francisco, CA

Not pictured

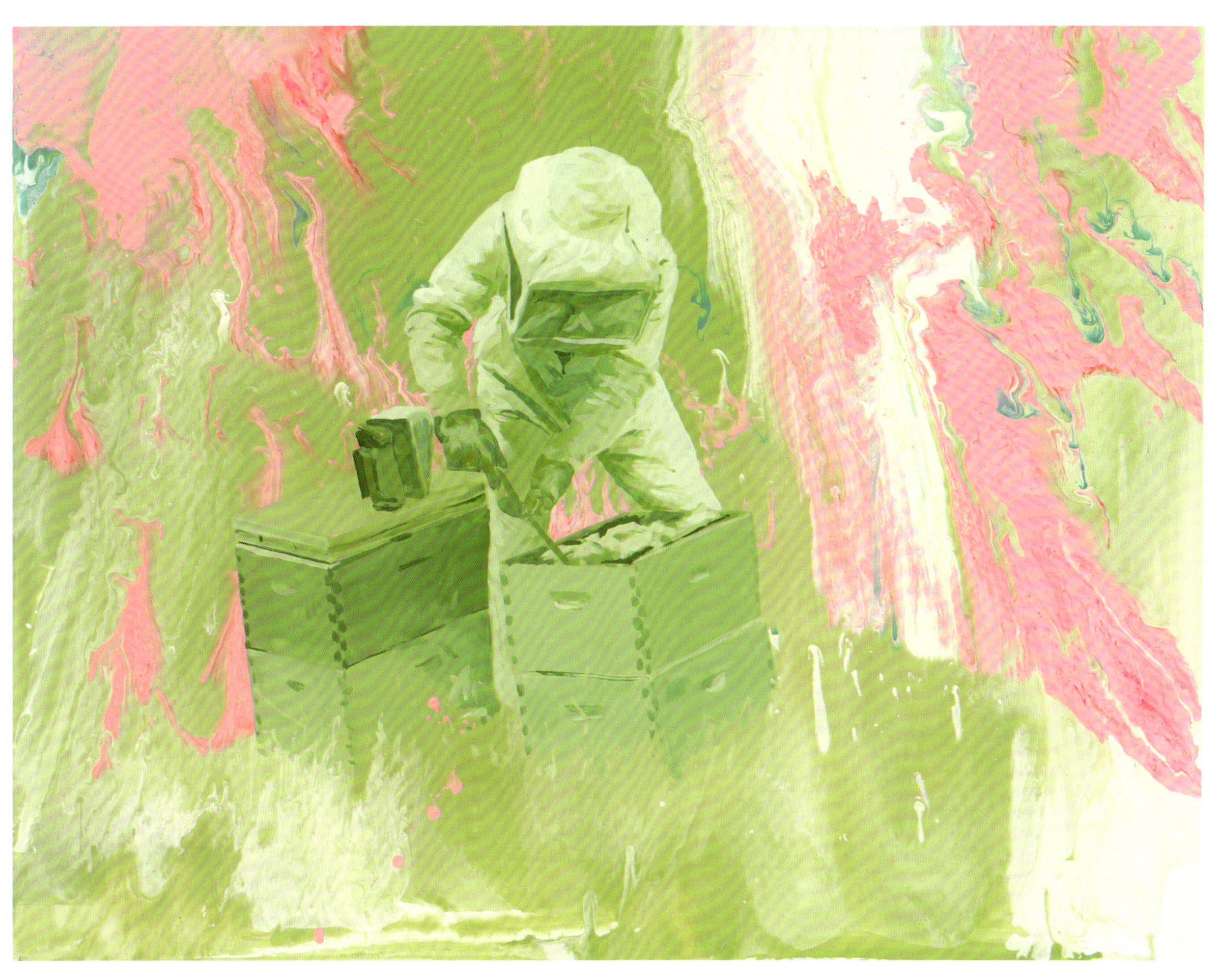

PLATE 21

Vert Veronese, 2003

Oil and enamel on linen

42 x 72 inches

Collection of Jeff & Karen Block, San Francisco, CA

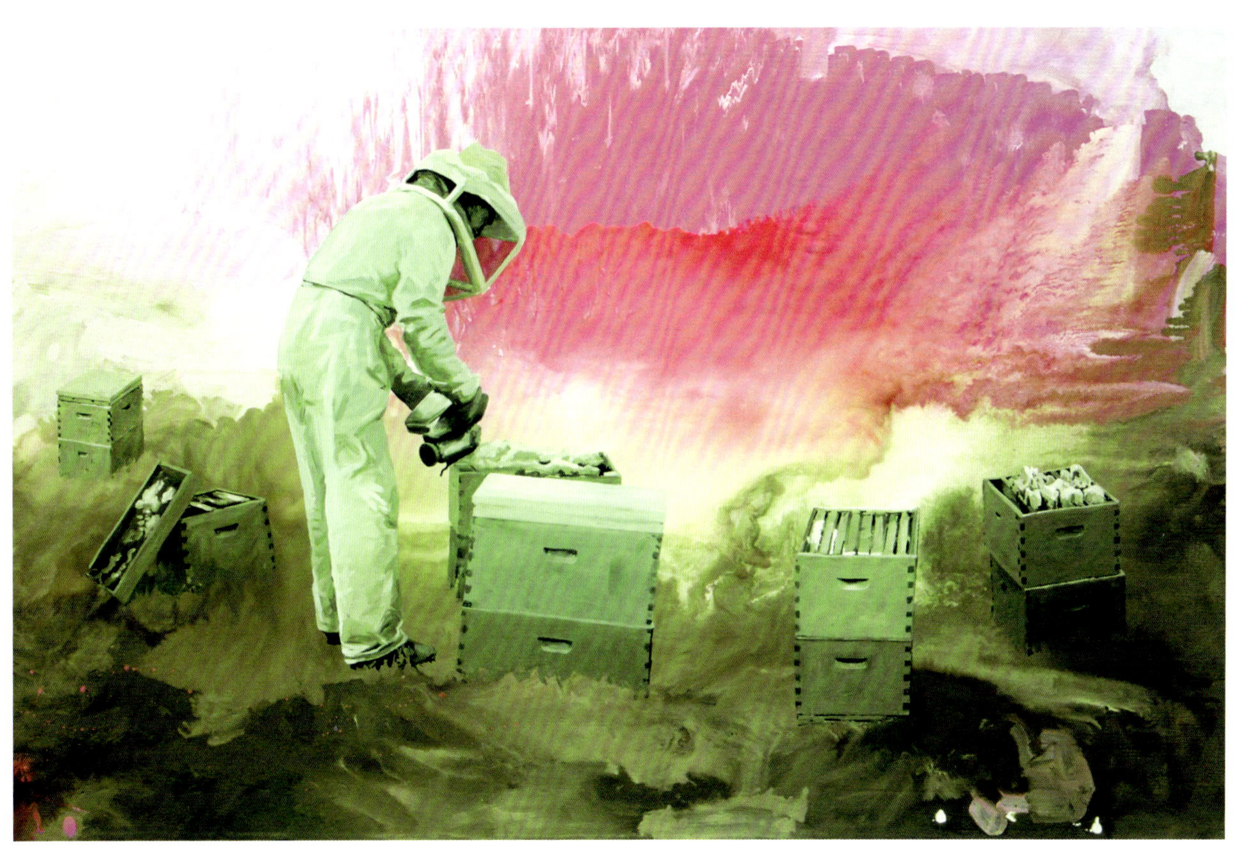

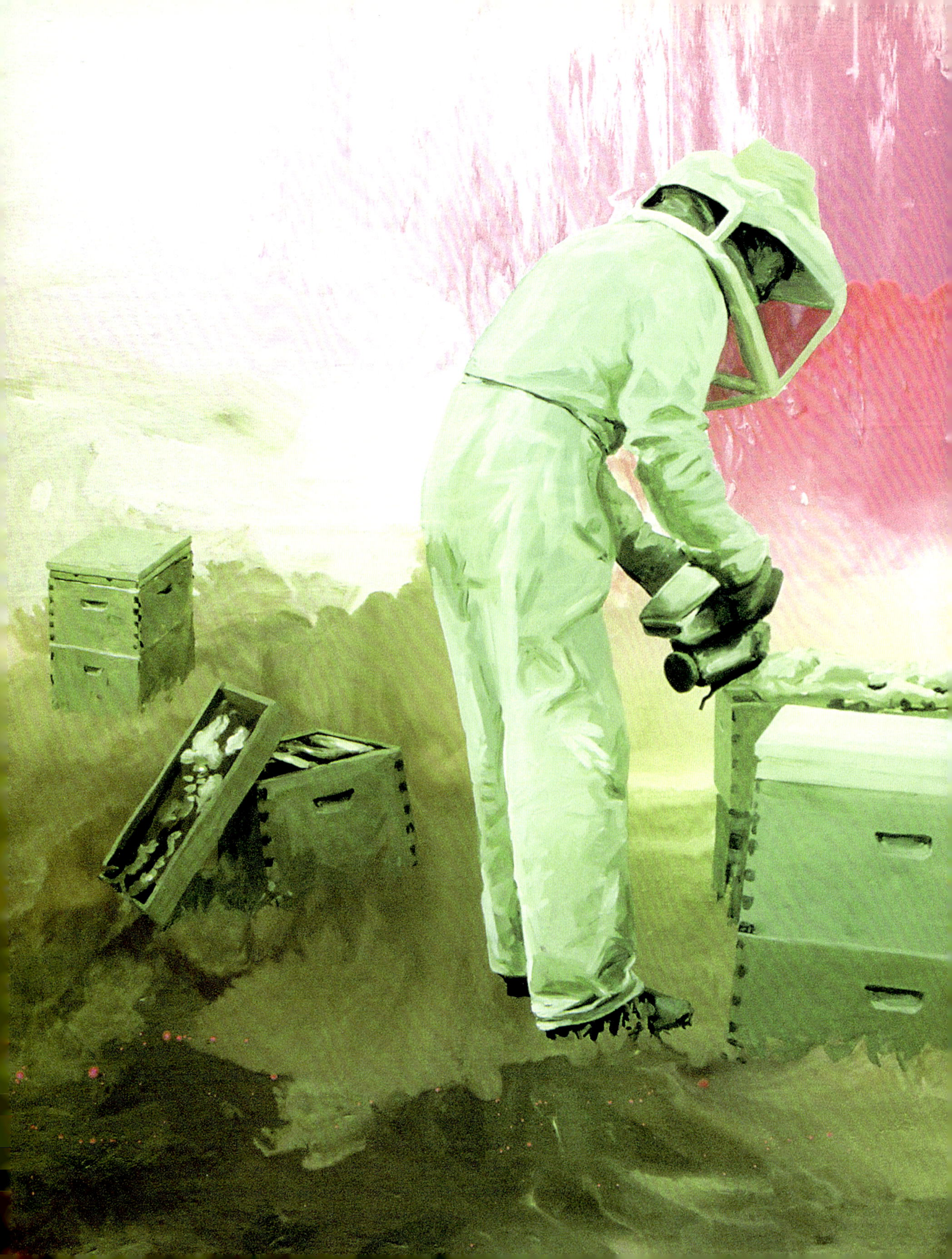

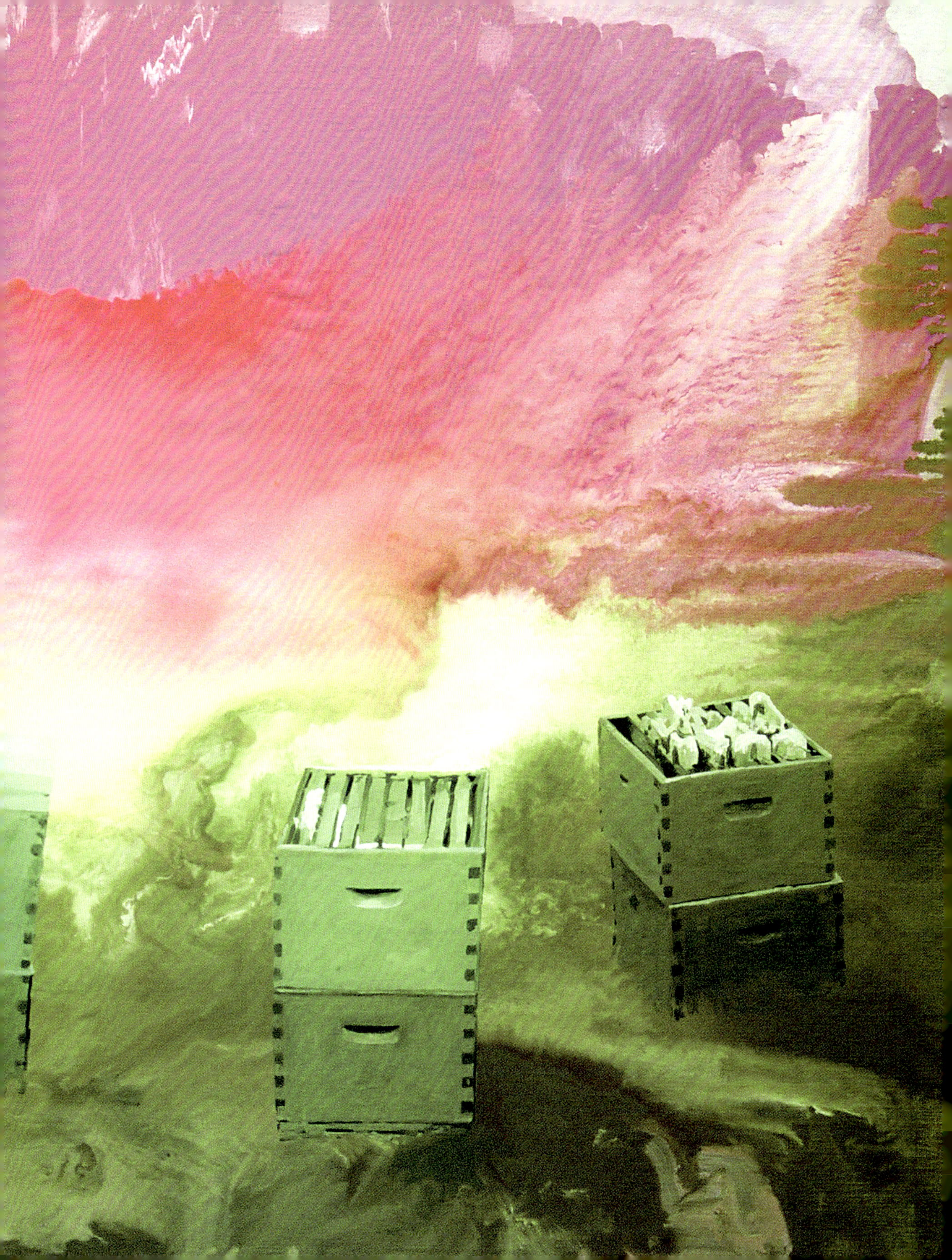

The Lure of Paris, #22, 2002

Oil on linen

72 x 72 inches

Courtesy of Sutton Gallery, Melbourne, Australia

Private colllection, Sydney, Australia

The Lure of Paris, #21, 2001

Oil on linen

72 x 72 inches

Courtesy of Sutton Gallery, Melbourne, Australia

Private colllection, Melbourne, Australia

Not pictured

The Lure of Paris, #15, 1999

Oil on linen

72 x 72 inches

Collection of Ellen & Jimmy Isenson, CA

Not pictured

The Lure of Paris, #11, 1998

Oil on linen

72 x 72 inches

Collection of John L. Stewart, New York, NY

Not pictured

The Lure of Paris, #9, 1997

Oil on linen

72 x 72 inches

Collection of John L. Stewart, New York, NY

Not pictured

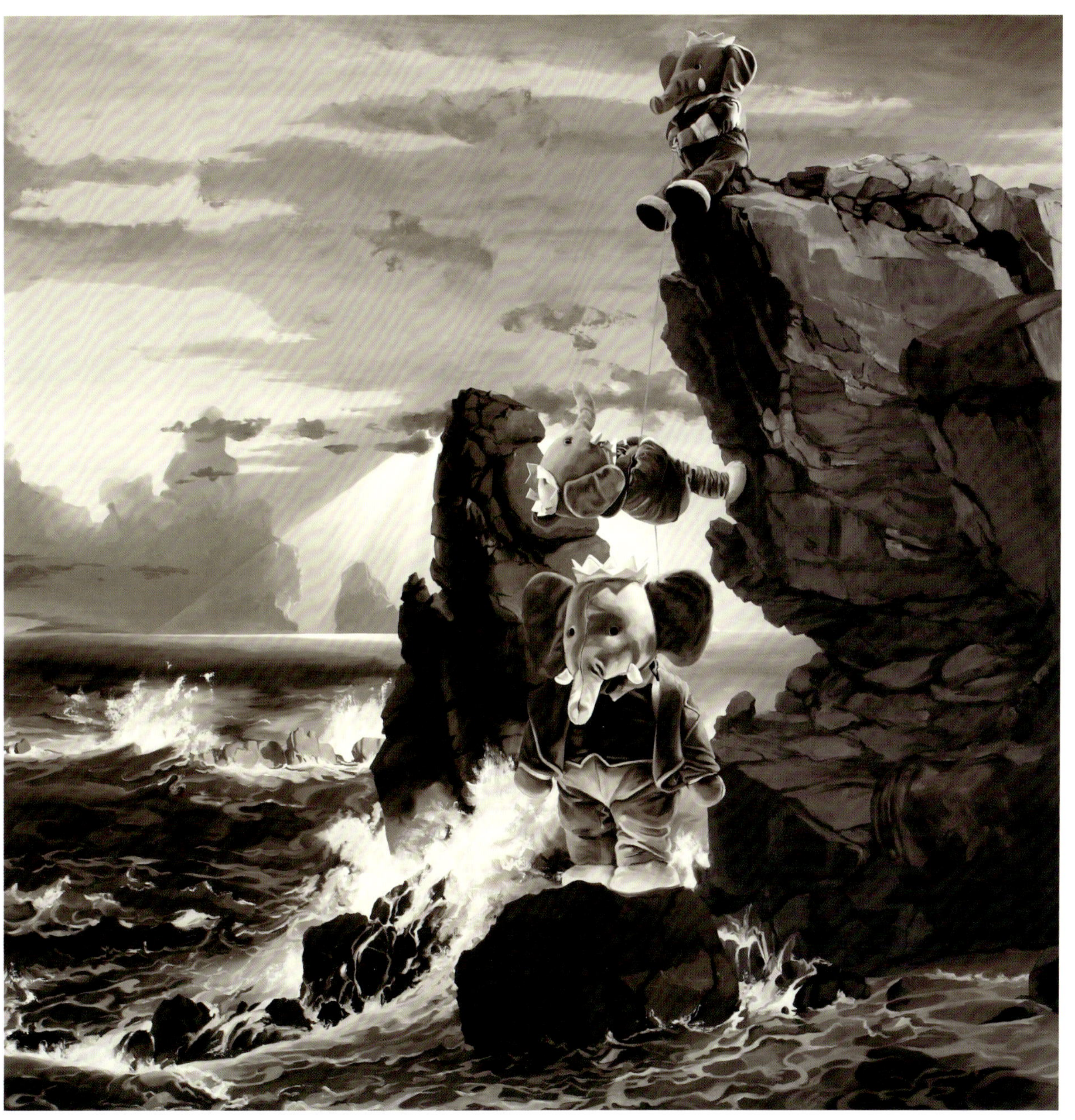

PLATE 23

A Caretaker #1, 1988

Oil on linen

24 x 28 inches

Collection of John L. Stewart, New York, NY

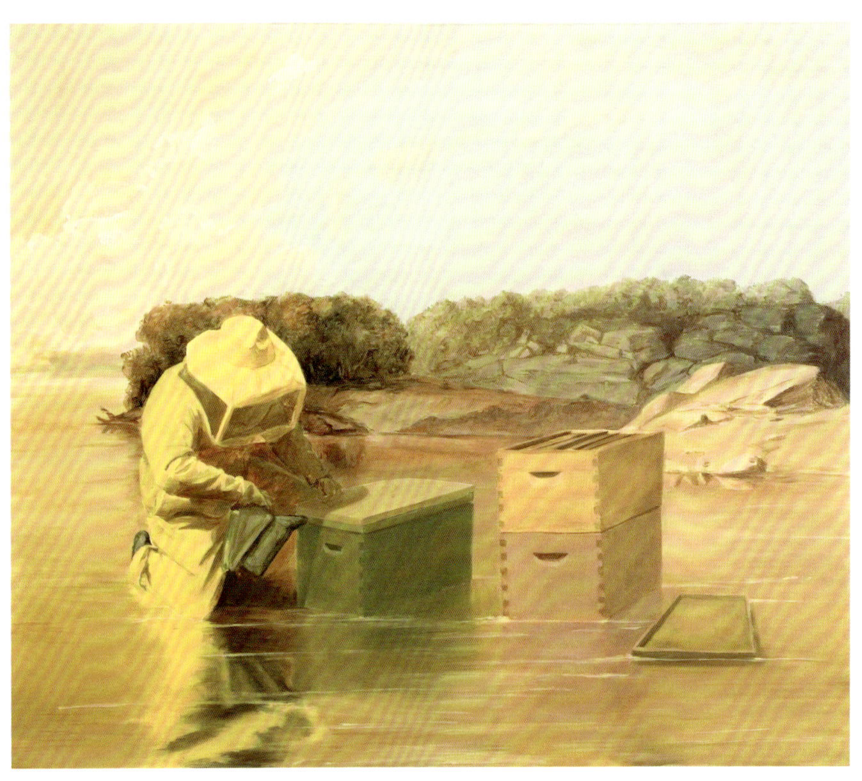

PLATE 24

A Caretaker #2, 1988

Oil on linen

28 x 24 inches

Collection of John L. Stewart, New York, NY

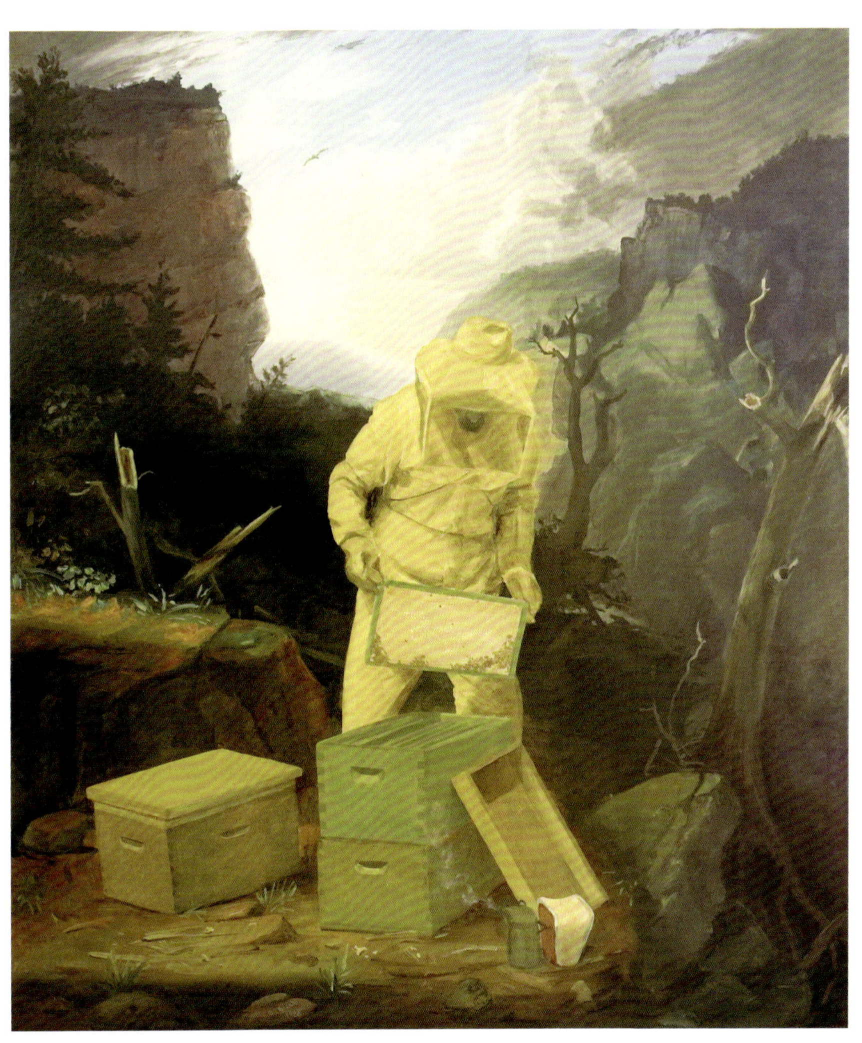

PLATE 25

A Caretaker #3, 1988

Oil on linen

24 x 28 inches

Collection of John L. Stewart, New York, NY

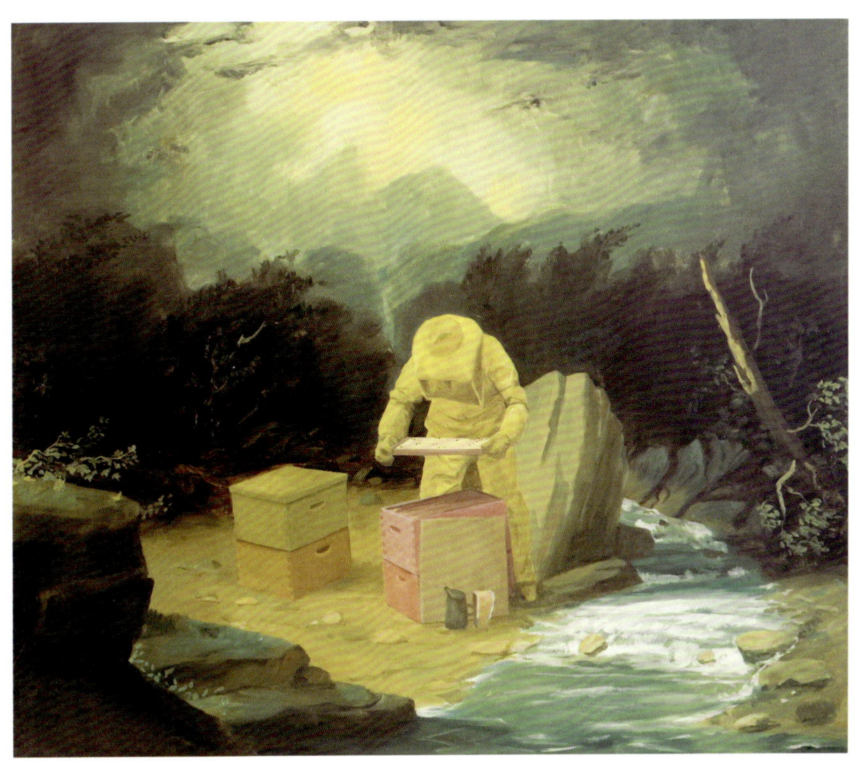

The Caretaker, 1988

Oil on linen

28 x 24 inches

Collection of John L. Stewart, New York, NY

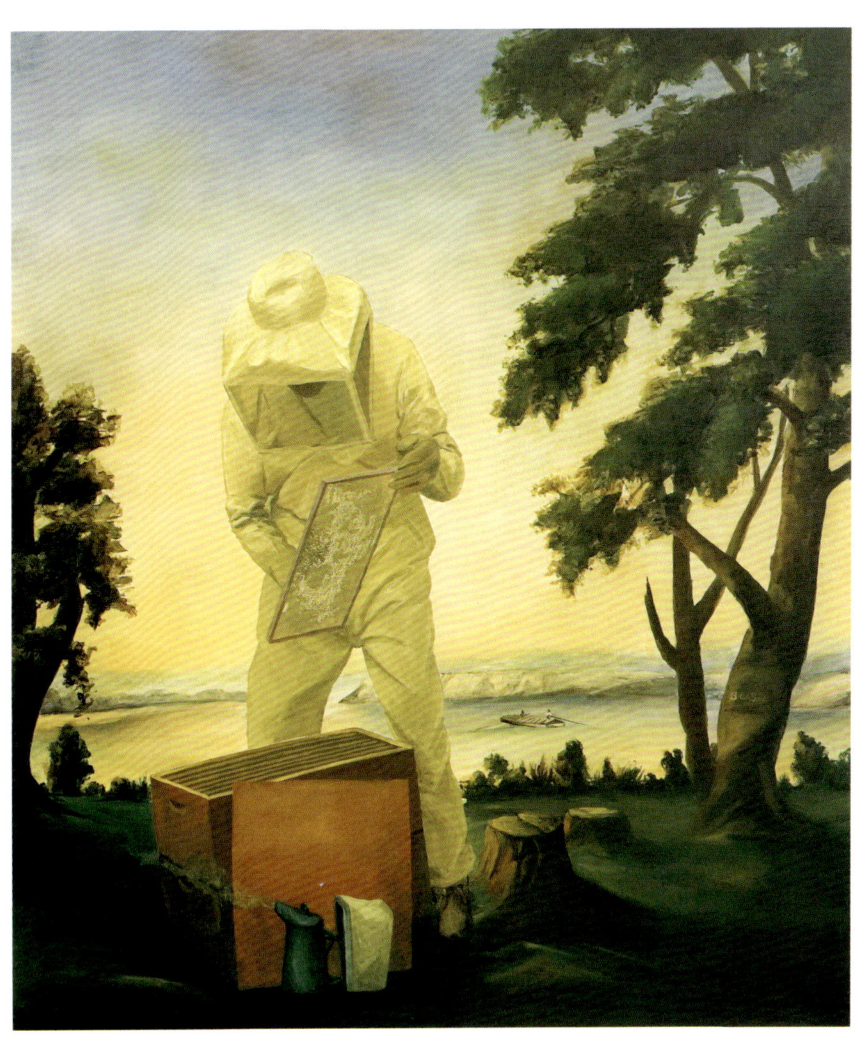

PLATE 27

Yellow, 1984

Oil on linen

48 x 78 inches

Collection, Wesfarmers, Perth, Australia

Not in exhibition

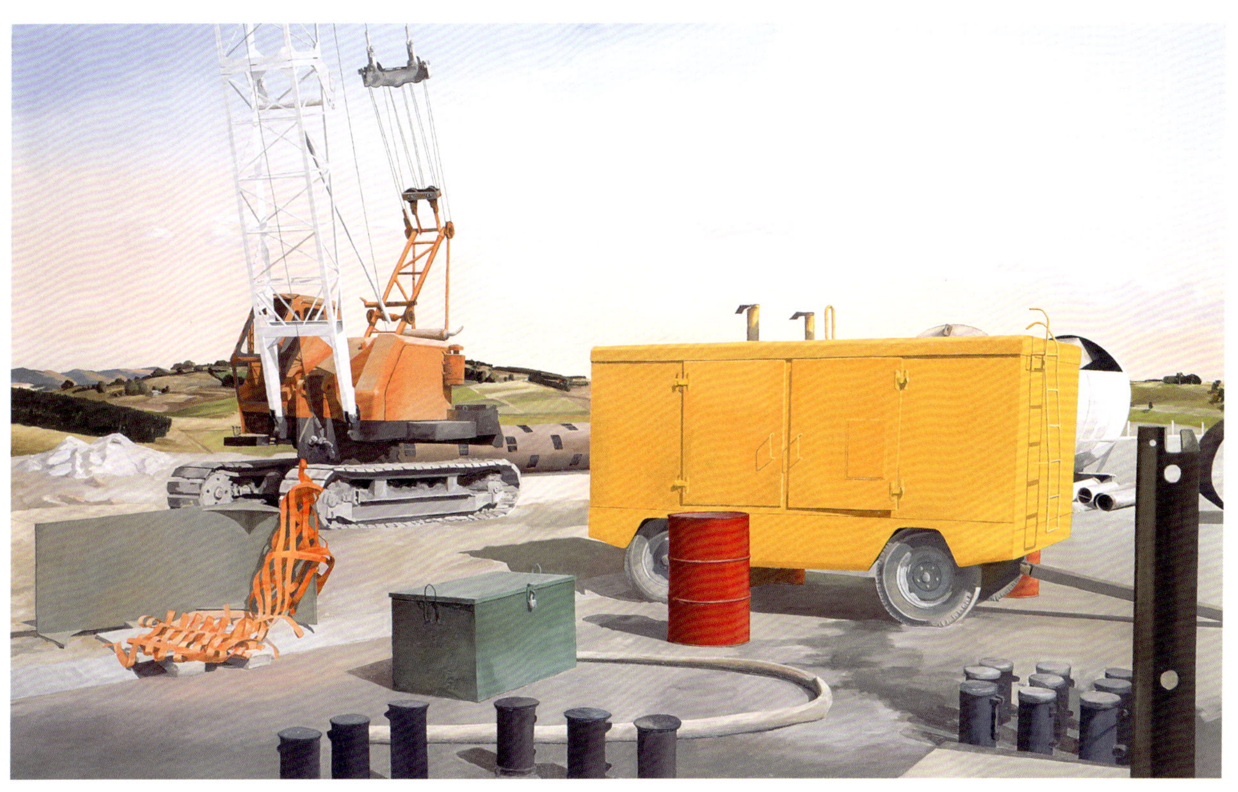

Stephen Bush would like to thank the following people for their assistance and support: Jan Nelson; Irene Sutton and gallery staff, in particular Phoebe Dougall for her diligence in realizing this project; Robert Goff and Cassie Rosenthal and gallery staff; Laura Heon and the team at SITE Santa Fe; the writers Ashley Crawford and Liza Statton for their insights; and all the owners that have generously lent their work.

acknowledgements

Stephen Bush: *Gelderland* is made possible, in part, by generous support from the Board of Directors of SITE Santa Fe as well as the following institutions and individuals:

The Brown Foundation, Inc., of Houston

The Burnett Foundation

The Ford Foundation — New Directions/New Donors for the Arts Initiative

New Mexico Arts, a division of the Department of Cultural Affairs, and the National Endowment for the Arts

Thaw Charitable Trust

The City of Santa Fe Arts Commission and the 1% Lodgers' Tax

Goff + Rosenthal, New York, NY

Sutton Gallery, Melbourne, Australia

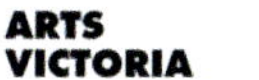

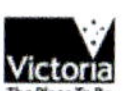

SITE Santa Fe Staff

Laura Steward Heon
Director/Curator

Tyler Auwarter
Director of Operations

David Renner
Operations Assistant

Carol Canfield
Volunteer Coordinator

Martha DeFoe
Guest Services Associate

Katy Hill
Visitor Services Manager & Education Assistant

Bill Hinsvark
Guest Services Associate

Joanne Lefrak
Curatorial Coordinator

Juliet Myers
Director of Education & Public Programs

Felicia A. Ponca
Events Manager

Catherine Putnam
Deputy Director & Chief Financial Officer

Michelle Ryals
Accountant & Human Resources Administrator

Jo-Anne Skinner
Membership & Travel Program Manager

Logan Staggs
Computer Technician

Liza Statton
Thaw Curatorial Fellow

Sally Wiseman
Development Manager

Anne Wrinkle
PR & Marketing Manager

Katia Zavistovski
Education Coordinator

SITE Guides:
Carol Canfield
Virginia Felix
Ai Krasner
Bradley Pecore
Clayton Porter
Tim Scott

Preparators:
Reanna Cool
Pam Ellison
Steven Fowler
Michael Gurule
Tim Jag
Ai Krasner
Clayton Porter
Alex Schmidt
Robert Slingsby
Spencer Stair

Exhibitions Intern:
Sage Sommer